THE
DAVID LINDSAY GILLESPIE
AND
ANNA RANDOLPH DARLINGTON GILLESPIE
READING ROOMS
CARNEGIE LIBRARY OF PITTSBURGH

WITHDRAWN FROM COLLECTION

L

Carnegie Library of Pittsburgh

Social Sciences Department

TOTTO-CHAN'S CHILDREN

TOTTO-CHAN'S CHILDREN

A Goodwill Journey to the Children of the World

Tetsuko Kuroyanagi

Translated by Dorothy Britton

```
HV873.K87 2000x

Kuroyanagi, Tetsuko,
1933-
Totto-chan's children :
a goodwill journey to
2000.
```

KODANSHA INTERNATIONAL
Tokyo • New York • London

A commemorative Tanzanian stamp issued in 1996 and featuring Tetsuko Kuroyanagi is reproduced on the front cover.
Jacket and cover design by Makoto Wada.
Photograph on page 161 by Ichiro Tagawa.
All other photographs by Takeyoshi Tanuma.

Distributed in the United States by Kodansha America, Inc., 575 Lexington Avenue, New York, New York 10022, and in the United Kingdom and continental Europe by Kodansha Europe Ltd., 95 Aldwych, London WC2B 4JF.

Published by Kodansha International Ltd., 17-14 Otowa 1-chome, Bunkyo-ku, Tokyo 112-8652, and Kodansha America, Inc. Originally published in 1997 in Japanese under the title *Totto-chan to totto-chan tachi* by Kodansha Ltd., Tokyo.

Copyright © 1997 by Tetsuko Kuroyanagi.
English translation copyright © 2000 by Kodansha International Ltd.
All rights reserved. Printed in Japan.
ISBN 4-7700-2532-7
First Edition, 2000

00 01 02 03 04 10 9 8 7 6 5 4 3 2 1

This book is dedicated to the 180 million children
who died from malnutrition, infectious disease
or civil war, always trusting the adults and
never grumbling about their situation,
in the thirteen years from when
I became a UNICEF goodwill
ambassador in 1984 until
1997. Rest in peace,
little ones.

Map 8
Prologue 11

Chapter One
TANZANIA, 1984 —— 17

Chapter Two
NIGER, 1985 —— 35

Chapter Three
INDIA, 1986 —— 47

Chapter Four
MOZAMBIQUE, 1987 —— 57

Chapter Five
CAMBODIA AND VIETNAM, 1988 —— 69

Chapter Six
ANGOLA, 1989 —— 89

Chapter Seven
BANGLADESH, 1990 —— 105

Chapter Eight
IRAQ, 1991 —— 121

Chapter Nine
ETHIOPIA, 1992 —— 135

Chapter Ten
SUDAN, 1993 —— 151

Chapter Eleven
RWANDA, 1994 —— 165

Chapter Twelve
HAITI, 1995 —— 179

Chapter Thirteen
BOSNIA-HERZEGOVINA, 1996 —— 193

Epilogue   211
Afterword 213
Postscript 219

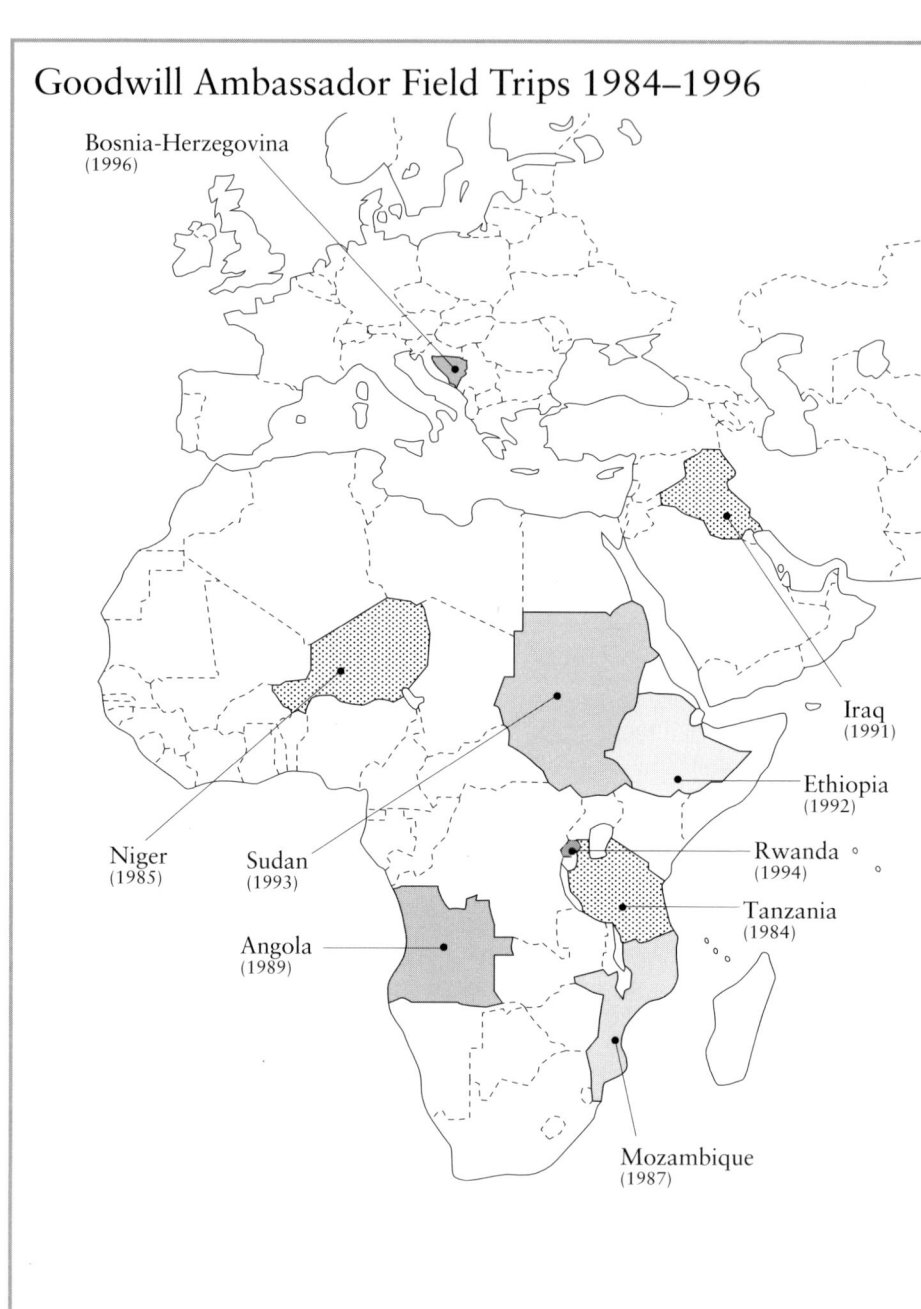

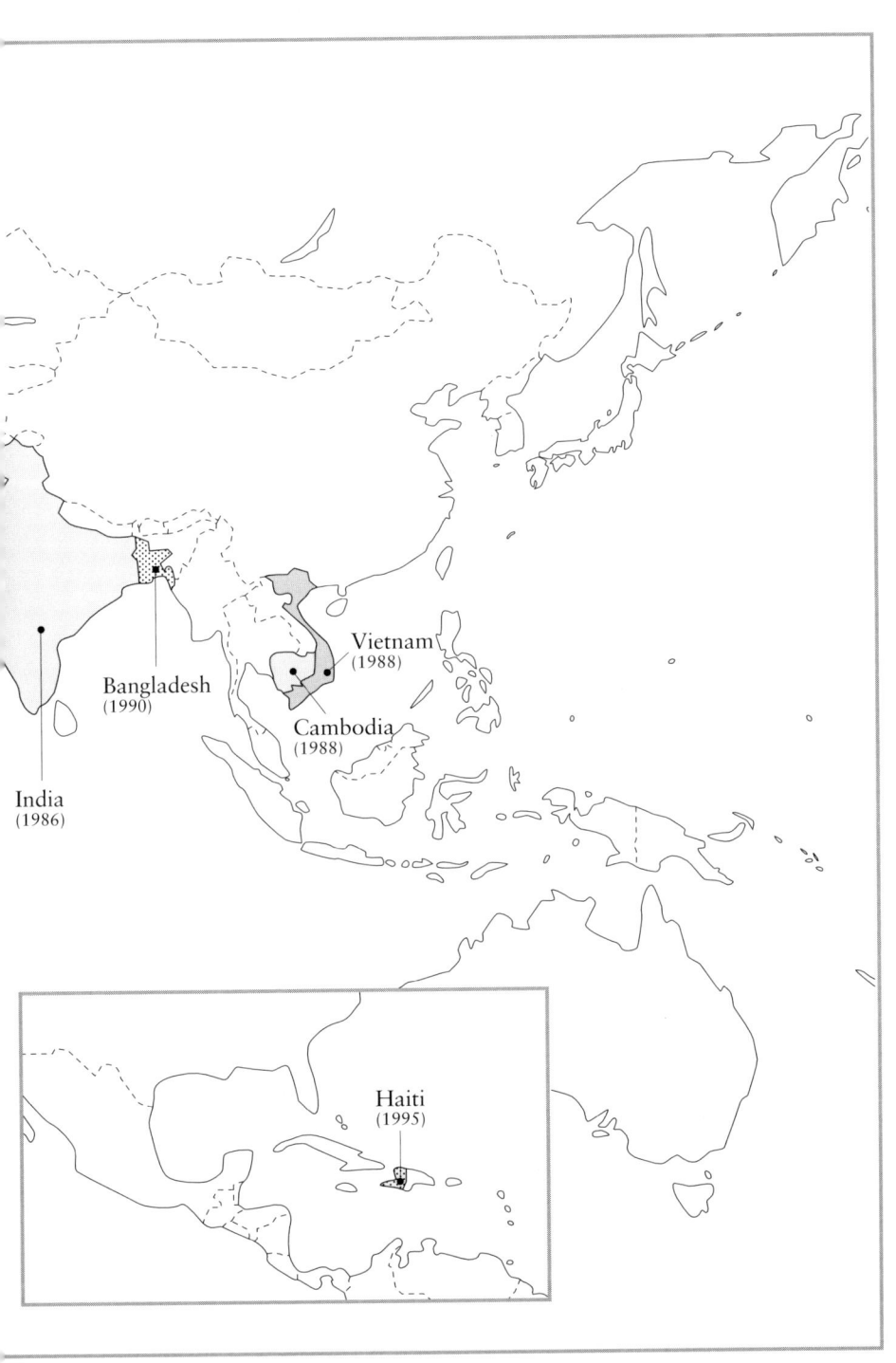

PROLOGUE

God Created Children Pure and Good
   A million people were killed in Rwanda.
   Little children fled, slipping through the massacre,
   Amid the shrieks and groans of the dying.
   Parents, sisters, brothers killed before their eyes
   And they knew not why,
   But just followed the fleeing grownups.
   And all those little children
   Bore a great grief in their tiny hearts,
   Thinking they were to blame
   For the death of their families!
   "I did things Mom said I mustn't do;
   That's why she was killed."
   "I must have done something really bad."
   It was actually the Hutus and the Tutsis
   Fighting each other,
   But the little children did not know that,
   So they all blamed themselves.
   Millions became refugees.
   Cholera broke out in the refugee camps;
   Every day thousands of adults and children died.
   By the road a little girl sat silently
   Beside her mother, who had died of cholera,
   And the child was thinking,
   "Mommy died because of me. Because she tried to save me."
   The children went on blaming themselves, like that,
   Convinced it was their fault.
   I'd never heard till then such things as this.
   Why would pure, innocent children

Chastise themselves like that when they were blameless?
I, who thought I knew something about children,
Was ashamed to find how little I knew.
Here in Japan today no one wants to take the blame
For any of our social ills.
Yet once we, too, were pure and innocent children.
I, as an adult, shall try never to forget
What those little children taught me.

The Words of a Tanzanian Village Chief

In a nameless village in Tanzania,
There were children unable to think or talk.
Brain-damaged from malnutrition,
They could not even walk. They could only crawl.
The elderly village chief said to me:
"Miss Kuroyanagi, when you return to Japan,
There is one thing I want you to remember:
Adults die groaning, complaining of their pain,
But children say nothing.
They simply die silently, under the banana leaves,
Trusting us adults."

In India,
I met a boy dying of tetanus.
I said to him softly, in Japanese:
"Cheer up, dear, the doctor is doing all he can for you."
The boy looked at me
With his beautiful, large eyes
And tried to say something.
Tetanus is a terrible disease:
The muscles stiffen and you cannot speak.
I asked the nurse what he had tried to say.
"I pray for your happiness," she translated.
I was too moved for words.
That dying boy made no complaint whatsoever.

He said only that.
Had he but been inoculated,
He need not have died.
The Tanzanian village chief's words
And those of that Indian boy
Will remain in my heart forever.

True Poverty Indeed

Seventy-two percent of prostitutes in Haiti
Have HIV, they said.
I asked one, who was only twelve years old,
"Aren't you afraid of AIDS?"
Her reply was straight, and to the point:
"Yes, I'm afraid, but even if I get it,
I'll stay alive a few years more, won't I?
Unless I work, there is no food for tomorrow."
Her few pennies each time would stave away
The family's starvation.

African Children Who Had Never Seen an Elephant

At a Tanzanian elementary school,
Our Japanese TV director
Handed out some drawing paper, saying,
"Draw an animal."
Handling such large white sheets of paper
For the first time in their lives,
The children seemed at a loss.
About an hour later,
"They have finished," announced the teacher.
Each child held high his work for me to see.
I was nonplussed.
Only two children had drawn animals.
One, a boy, had drawn, in the corner of his sheet,

PROLOGUE

A single fly.
Another boy had made a primitive attempt
To draw a bird with spindly legs.
That was all. The other children
Drew buckets, tea cups, and the like.
We had imagined
African children would draw lively pictures
Of elephants, giraffes and zebras.
But then, even in Africa, animals
Only inhabit certain areas
That are specially protected.
The children who live there
Probably know about the animals.
But for most of the children,
There are no zoos, no television
And no picture books.
So that even though they live in Africa,
They know nothing about the continent's animals.
And yet, Japanese children,
Although they live so far away,
Would have no problem drawing an elephant.
And they know what a zebra is.
Will those African children
Live their whole lives, and die,
Without ever knowing about Africa's animals?

I had always longed to visit Africa.
I used to imagine giraffes
Etched against a sunset sky.
I still have not seen the animals of Africa.
The places I go,
Places where children are in need of help,
Have no water and very little greenery.
They have civil wars.
They are not places where animals can live;
People cannot live there.
Even in Japan, in wartime,

Food became scarce and
The animals in zoos had to be killed.
Elephants would perform tricks,
Thinking that would bring them food;
They were killed doing their balancing acts.
Japanese children ought to know
That elephants can only be seen
Where there is prosperity and peace.
I wished with all my heart
They could be taught that.

Children Targeted in the Bosnia-Herzegovina War

Deep in my heart I thought,
That is one thing I could never forgive:
Setting up a bomb
In a child's beloved stuffed toy.
Children adore stuffed toys.

As a child in World War II,
I never ran to the air-raid shelter
Without my teddy bear.
I wanted to take it with me
When we were evacuated.
Daddy had given it to me
When he left for the army;
It was my friend.
My mother made me leave the teddy bear behind.
The train was crowded, and
She had two small children with her.
We weren't allowed any baggage.
I was terribly unhappy.
As we went out of the house,
I left my gray teddy bear on Daddy's chair.
When I heard the house had burned,
The first thing I thought of,

PROLOGUE

The very first thing,
Was my teddy bear.
I pictured it
Enveloped in flames.
So that's how I know
How precious stuffed toys
Are to children.

Fighting broke out in Bosnia.
Roofs were blown off;
People ran hither and yon,
Trying to escape,
Always protecting the children.
As soon as fighting subsided
People returned to their homes.
One little girl went to her room,
Straight to her beloved stuffed toy.
"Sorry I couldn't take you with me.
Thank you for waiting," she may have said,
Picking it up to hug it.
That is when the bomb went off,
Killing the child.

While the house was empty
One of the enemy went in
And hid a bomb inside the stuffed toy
So it would explode when clasped.
To think that even child psychology
Is made use of in war!
What must that child have thought
As she died, hugging her stuffed toy?
Was it, "How could you do this to me?
You were my friend."
Oh, how I hate war!

Chapter One

TANZANIA, 1984

By the beginning of the 1980s, fourteen million children under the age of five were dying each year; that is, about forty thousand every day. Because of starvation, insanitary conditions, and the lack of inoculations, children contracted infectious diseases or suffered from diarrhea, and died. Many children were killed, too, as a result of being caught up in wars; in particular, civil war.

I was appointed goodwill ambassador for UNICEF (the acronym stands for United Nations International Children's Emergency Fund, now abbreviated to United Nations Children's Fund), in 1984. There were daily reports in the newspapers and on television about famine in Africa. But, at that time, the news meant little to people in faraway Japan. I therefore asked UNICEF if I could go to Africa for my first tour, and it was decided that I should visit Tanzania. At the time, the country's population was about twenty million. Its area is 364,900 square miles.

Tanzania had suffered a severe drought; and without any rain since 1981, almost no grain could be grown. Every day, nearly six hundred children under the age of five were dying of starvation and disease.

I thought I understood a good deal about the starving children in Africa, having seen television programs, books of photographs and documentary films on the subject, all showing skin-and-bones children with their ribs sticking out. Moreover, I myself had been through a war in which food became scarce and I became so thin and undernourished that my body was covered with sores. And there were children I knew—the same age as I was—who died of malnutrition. So I thought I knew something about starvation.

But the real starvation I saw in Tanzania with my own eyes was a terrible thing indeed.

Giyon

I met a six-year-old boy in Tanzania called Rogati. Normally a boy that age would be in elementary school, but he was very small and could neither stand, nor walk, nor talk. All he could do was crawl about on the cold earth. That is what starvation does. When a child gets no nourishment, not only the body but the brain is stunted as well, for it, too, needs nourishment. I had no idea that starvation was so abhorrent. It was a great shock to me.

When the little boy saw me, he hurriedly crawled over to me, dug a handful of mud with his tiny fingers and held it out to me, saying, "*giyon*." I thought this must be a word in Swahili, but the UNICEF representative who was with me said it didn't mean anything. I was told that the boy's brain damage was incurable, that even giving him food at this stage would have no positive effect on his condition. No matter how long he lived, he would never be able to do anything but crawl. It was pitiful to think that the boy's condition was due only to lack of food.

Since Rogati wore no pants and crawled about on the earth with his bare legs exposed, his hands and feet were ice cold. One thinks of Africa as being hot, but here, near Mount Kilimanjaro, which rises 19,170 feet above sea level, it gets quite cold. All I could do for that child was hold his hands between my own and try to warm them.

Rogati seemed to look right inside me with his enormous eyes. He kept on repeating, "*giyon, giyon*." That was the only thing he could say.

Rogati's mother, aged thirty, carried a two-year-old son in her arms, but she said he had not uttered a single word since he was born. She, herself, was so undernourished that she had scarcely any milk. Powdered milk was unavailable, and of course there was no

TANZANIA, 1984

Rogati, who gave me some mud, saying, "giyon."

cow's milk. All newborn babies had to drink was tea or water, which contain no nourishment at all.

Two girls stood near me, aged seven and nine. They were small for their age, too, and their heads were covered with sores.

Rogati's father had disappeared about a year before.

Flavorless bananas were the staple food. Hoping to be able to obtain some coarsely ground corn as well, Rogati's mother worked at a farmhouse in the neighborhood. She also had to look after her husband's parents, who lived six miles away. It seemed to me that the position of women differed little from that of women in Japan in the old days.

The small mud hut that was home to Rogati and his family had no windows and was pitch dark. There was no kitchen.

As for food, the family had had nothing but tea that day. I felt it was a rather cruel question to ask, but said, "If you could eat anything you liked right now, what would it be?"

The mother thought for a moment, then replied, "Thick corn porridge. Really thick."

"And I'd like to give the children something to eat at least once a day," she added. The only thing they had in the house was a dried fish that looked half rotten.

It was the same at the house next door. There were six children, all thin with distended bellies and light brown hair—both signs of extreme malnutrition. Healthy black children have black, curly hair. Malnutrition, on the other hand, causes the hair to become straggly and pale, so it looks as if it is covered in dust or light brown earth.

The children's mother, who looked exhausted, said, "I can't remember when we last had a really good meal."

The baby in her arms was crying, but it did not make a sound. And when I looked more closely, I could see that its head and its arms were a mass of wrinkles. And those wrinkles were not fine little wrinkles, but deep furrows, like pleats.

That night, when I returned to the lodge at the foot of Kilimanjaro, Africa's highest mountain, I could not sleep for sadness. I kept hearing that clear voice repeating the word *giyon*.

"Miss Kuroyanagi, when you return to Japan, there is just one thing I want you to remember: Adults die groaning, complaining of their pain, but children say nothing. They simply die silently, under the banana leaves, trusting us adults."

These words, too—spoken by the village chief of that tiny nameless Tanzanian hamlet—kept returning to me.

But They Really *Were* Crying

I visited a small clinic where about twenty small children and babies were sitting or lying about on the concrete floor. Suddenly, I realized there was no sound at all of children crying.

I pointed this out to the man from TV Asahi—a Japanese broadcasting company—who was with me.

Without taking his eyes from the viewfinder of the heavy camera he was carrying, the cameraman replied, "No, the microphone isn't picking up any sound at all."

Twenty small children one and two years old, all in one place, separated from their parents and sick from malnutrition: normally, more than a few would be crying fretfully. But in this clinic, the children simply did not have the strength to cry.

It was the first time I had come across such a spectacle: a whole crowd of children not making a sound. When improperly fed, children become lethargic and indifferent and can only sit and stare. But these children, though they made no sound, really *were* crying. You could tell, because their enormous eyes were filled with tears.

Aside from tears, the children's eyes were also covered with flies. Flies clung to the babies' mouths, too, trying to suck up nourishment from their tears, their noses and their little mouths.

I couldn't bear to see those flies and kept trying to shoo them away with my hands. The children themselves did not even have the strength to do so and just let the insects crawl about their faces.

When the flies left and I could see the children's faces clearly, it was hard to have those beautiful, large eyes staring at me, knowing there was nothing I could do. Oh, if only there was something I could do for you, I thought, as I hugged them. Yet even when I dandled them they did not smile. It takes nourishment to be able to even smile. All the infants could do was stare at me in silence. This notwithstanding, every child I held invariably clutched at my dress. It was as if they were trying to tell me they liked being hugged. The children were starving not only for food but for love as well.

Benedicta

While visiting all sorts of places in Tanzania, many of the sights I saw were heartrending, but I never allowed myself to cry. For one thing, I felt it would be rude and, at any rate, there was no time for tears.

There was one occasion, however, when I couldn't help crying. I was visiting an orphanage at the foot of Kilimanjaro. It was an orphanage run by Catholic volunteers from Europe. Built of wood and fitted with glass windows, the orphanage was clean and bright, in contrast to the typical window-less mud-hut homes of this area.

The orphanage housed some fifty children, from babies up to about the age of six. Some of the children were healthy. Others, such as those who had been abandoned because they were blind from malarial fever, were not.

Since children living with their parents often had to go hungry, some people said the orphans were better off because they had, at least, a little to eat. What can be sadder, though, than being without any family when one is so small? I felt real pity for the orphans and played with the little ones, talked to the older ones in a language they could not understand, and joined them all when they had their meals.

The nun who ran the orphanage took me into a room where there were about ten three-year-olds.

"*Jambo*," I said, which means "hello." They all watched me inquisitively from a distance and then gradually began to come over to where I sat on the wooden floor. Some were brave enough to touch me, then ran back with a little scream. They were all quite adorable.

I noticed a little girl of about two and a half, in a green dress, standing in the corner all by herself, looking at me.

"Come and join us," I said in Japanese, holding out my arms. But she did not move.

By this time, the other children were pulling at my dress and climbing onto my lap. No matter how much I urged the little girl in green to join us, she would not come.

After that, I visited other rooms and watched a dance. Later, when I happened to pass the same room again, there was the girl in the green dress standing motionless in exactly the same spot.

"Do come!" I called. But she did not move. So I went and joined the other children.

The third time I passed the room, I went in and sat on the floor and said to the girl, "I have to go now." And the little girl in the green dress suddenly rushed over to me and jumped onto my lap. The Sister who was behind me whispered, "Miss Kuroyanagi, this is a miracle! Ever since she was brought here, this child hasn't spoken a word or gone near anyone. She has just kept to herself. This is the first time she has approached anyone. There's no other explanation for it. It is a miracle!"

The child's name was Benedicta. Her family was terribly poor, the father had disappeared and her mother was beset with such trials that she lost her mind. A man who said he was her uncle had brought her to the orphanage as a baby. According to the Sister, he was never seen again.

Benedicta made herself thoroughly at home on my lap and lay there for ages, just like a pussycat. Then she put both her arms around my neck and clung to me with her legs. She wouldn't let go, so I carried her in my arms as I continued my tour of the orphanage.

The time finally came for me to leave. It was nearly evening. We went outside, and I put Benedicta down. Stooping, I sat on my heels in the road and said to her "I have to go now."

All of a sudden, she put her face right up against mine and clasped my head with her arms.

When people part from their loved ones, they usually hug one another, lay cheek against cheek, or kiss in the case of adults. But Benedicta knew nothing of these ways, so she simply pushed her face frontally into mine, and stayed like that indefinitely, without a word, clasping my head with all the strength a two-and-a-half-year-old girl could muster. It was all I could do to breathe.

This child, who had been unable to become attached to anyone, couldn't seem to bear parting from me. She had just been enduring her loneliness all this time. How wretchedly lonely she must have been. She probably had wanted so badly to be hugged.

Two and a half is not much more than a baby. When I thought about how little she was, I suddenly started to cry. When she finally let go, Benedicta's cheeks were wet with my tears. My cheeks, too, were covered with stuff from Benedicta's eyes and nose.

Holding her away from me I saw indeed how very small she was.

The Sister picked Benedicta up in her arms. "Bye-bye," said the Sister, as I stood up.

I wish I could have taken Benedicta home with me. She had been waiting so long for someone to love her.

In Turn, In Turn!

I visited the Dodoma area of Tanzania at the height of a severe drought. They had not had a drop of rain for eight months, and there was not a blade of grass as far as the eye could see. The fields of maize, like everything else, were withered and dry. The ground felt dry and powdery, even eight inches deep, and the dust kept blowing in the wind. There was no moisture anywhere.

A kind lady offered me some water from a small pan to wash my hands with. The water was muddy and looked like *café au lait*. I asked her where she got the water.

"From the well back there," she replied.

I went around to the back of the house to see, but couldn't find the well there.

"You said it was at the back...," I began.

"Three miles back," she explained.

I was stunned. She had given me precious water, albeit muddy, carried from three miles away.

TANZANIA, 1984

Digging a hole in a dried-up riverbed, the children wait for the hole to fill with water. After drinking a little of the water, they put the rest in pots to take home.

My guide, a lady member of the National Parliament from Dodoma, said to me, "Three miles is not so far. Some people have to walk as far as nine or ten miles. They are lucky to be able to get water at all, otherwise they wouldn't be able to live."

Children carrying pots of water on their heads against a vast, parched landscape may make a charming photograph, but fetching water is hard work, and children's work at that. The children must walk three miles, if the source is "near," and as much as six miles, if not, their search for water taking them across arid wastes to a stream or communal well.

The children work very hard indeed. They fetch water, gather firewood, and mind their younger brothers and sisters. Elementary school is supposed to be compulsory, but many children cannot go to school because there is too much work for them to do at home.

Soon after I left the Dodoma area, our car suddenly began shaking and bouncing about. The driver explained that the road we were driving along was the dried-up bed of what was once a large river. As we followed its winding course, with not a drop of water in sight, it presented a forbidding landscape.

I got out of the car at a spot where some children were digging for water. The well was so far off that if they became thirsty on the way there, this was all they could do. The children showed me how to dig a hole with their hands in the dirt of the riverbed, about twelve inches deep and sixteen inches wide. After a while, lo and behold, the bottom of the hole began to get wet. One had to wait patiently while the hole slowly filled up with water. In about ten minutes, there was enough to fill two small bowls. With practiced skill, the children first skimmed off the surface dust and debris. Still, half the water was mud. What amazed me was the way the children observed a rule of letting the younger ones drink first. "In turn, in turn!" the older ones would say. I was moved to see their thoughtfulness in spite of those dreadful conditions. The children gulped down the water with gusto.

Here in Japan we take it for granted that water gushes out of the tap. I had never stopped to think how fortunate we are. Filled with shame for my ignorance, I watched those well-behaved children taking their turns drinking the muddy water that they had dug up with their own hands.

Plan A, Plan B, Plan C

Wherever I went, water was a principal concern. In Moshi, I met Dr. Shangali, the passionate leader of the local council. He was an engineer.

"I want you to see our dam," he said. And so, early one morning,

I set out and was surprised to find, not the sort of dam I expected, but a medium-sized marsh. He scooped up a cup of the water. It was half mud, and there were tadpoles swimming about in it. Dr. Shangali said people and animals often fall into the water, but that its center is so deep that it is impossible to rescue them. As a result, their decomposing corpses remain in the water.

The water from the dam is piped to the village for drinking without any purification treatment. People are instructed to boil it, but thirsty children often just go ahead and drink it and then fall ill—with cholera, dysentery and other infectious diseases—and die.

Dr. Shangali opened up a document that I immediately recognized as a blueprint and spread it out before me.

"This is Mount Kilimanjaro," he said, pointing. "What I want to do is to bring its pure, unpolluted melted-snow water to the children, for them to drink. My plan is to pipe the water from this point at the foot of the mountain. I estimate that there will be enough drinking water for twenty thousand people. This is my Plan A route. That is my Plan B route. And this one is Plan C. UNICEF has already sent me the pipes. But they need to be securely joined together and buried in the ground. And finally, we will need a pump."

After we had left the dam and were on the way to the next stop, bouncing along in the jeep, Dr. Shangali unfolded the large blueprint again, with much rustling of paper. "This is Plan A, those are Plans B and C," he began again, saying finally, "I hope you have understood." This went on all day.

We visited a lot of places and, afterwards, in the jostling jeep, he would invariably bring out that blueprint again, unfold it with much rustling, and show me Plan A, Plan B and Plan C, saying, "I do hope you have understood." Plan A, Plan B and Plan C were even unfolded on the table where we had lunch.

Dr. Shangali's enthusiasm was such that at last I felt obliged to ask how much his scheme would cost.

"According to my calculations," he said, "I think it could be done for roughly two hundred thousand dollars."

By the time I had traveled all day in the jostling jeep with Dr. Shangali, I had become so used to his "Plan A, Plan B and Plan C" that once, when my eyes met his, I preempted him. "Plan A, Plan B and Plan C," I offered, and he smiled.

We reached the airport from where we were to return to the capital, Dar es Salaam. In the departure lounge, he once again unfolded the rustling sheet of paper and spread it out.

"It's really time to say farewell now," he said. "I do hope you will not forget Plan A, Plan B and Plan C, which I have explained to you."

Dr. Shangali's passionate desire to bring water to the children was firmly engraved upon my heart as I waved good-bye.

About two months after I returned to Japan, I received a letter from him:

> It was so kind of you to come and see conditions in Tanzania. We are most grateful. I have sent you some Kilimanjaro coffee to bring back memories of our country. I hope very much that you have not forgotten Plan A, Plan B and Plan C.

About ten days later, a parcel was delivered to me whose packing was so badly damaged it is a wonder that it arrived at all. It contained a tin of coffee decorated with a giraffe pattern. A couple of months after that, another letter arrived from Dr. Shangali:

> I hope the coffee I sent you arrived safely, and it will bring back to you memories of Kilimanjaro.

He added a postscript reminding me again not to forget Plan A, Plan B and Plan C.

On my return to Japan, I immediately spoke on television about the starvation and drought in Tanzania. The journalists who accompanied me also wrote about it in their respective newspapers and magazines. I was astounded at the amount of the donations sent to my UNICEF Goodwill Ambassador Account. One hundred and thirty million yen (1.3 million dollars) had been collected in the twinkling of an eye. I was thrilled. It had come from tiny kindergarten children, from old-age pensioners, and many wonderfully kind people. As the donors sent money because they had watched my program, I asked UNICEF to use the donations mainly for the places I had visited. I also asked the organization to send some of the funds to Dr. Shangali for his Plan A, Plan B and Plan C.

UNICEF does not just send countries money. They first send specialists and researchers to those places to see what is actually needed there. They determine, for instance, just how many people will benefit from a water pipeline. When they studied Dr. Shangali's Plan A, Plan B and Plan C, they found that his estimate of two hundred thousand dollars would not nearly be enough. They also said that to protect the lives and health of the children of that region it was not enough simply to make water available.

More children die in that region than any other in Tanzania, where some six hundred children die every day. Of the donations, forty million yen (four hundred thousand dollars) will be used in a general hygiene and sanitation operation directed toward the water supply. Dr. Shangali has sent me a letter asking me to say thank you on his behalf to the people of Japan.

When you tell Japanese children there are children in the world who have no water to drink, a lot of them say, "Why can't they drink canned fruit juice?" or "Why don't they buy mineral water?" I hope when young people read this book, they will realize what a precious thing water is. The children I met in my travels had never seen a bottle, nor a can of juice, nor any other drink, ever, in their lives.

The President Had Been a Headmaster!

I visited a number of elementary schools. They had hardly any teaching materials, no notebooks and no pencils. Rather, the pupils used chalk and little wooden boards to learn how to write and do sums. Only the teacher had a textbook.

As I mentioned in the Prologue, it was here that I discovered that there were children who, although they lived in Africa, had never seen an elephant, a lion or a giraffe.

At one school, the children had so little equipment that the teacher explained addition by scratching sums in the dust with a stick, while the children called out the answers.

That is how I learned that with appropriate application and sufficient will it is always possible to study. Tanzania's then-president, Julius Nyerere, was formerly a headmaster. It must have been at his instigation that the country's elementary schools also held classes for adults who had not had the chance to study when they were children. The adult classes were held at the same time as those for children. The sight of these adults, both male and female, earnestly studying arithmetic and history as well as reading and writing, was intensely moving.

If one can at least read and write, there are so many kinds of work one can do. Japan is said to have almost one hundred percent literacy, but there are many developing countries where only fifteen or twenty percent of the people can read. I was told that under Nyerere's leadership, Tanzania's literacy had risen to seventy percent. A great achievement. Nevertheless, one has to travel to the individual countries to understand that it is not laziness but poverty that witholds the chance of an education from so many people on this earth.

I met President Nyerere. He was a charming, dashing, high-spirited man of sixty-two. He had read the English translation of my *Totto-chan: The Little Girl at the Window*, and said, jokingly, "If you liked the headmaster of your elementary school, you'll probably like me, because I was a headmaster, too!"

The president was known affectionately as *Mwalimu*, "teacher." He told me he would much rather be addressed as that than as president. It was because of Nyerere's efforts that the literacy rate had risen so high in his country, long a colony of the British, who did not do much for its colony in the way of education.

The president invited me to his residence, where I was particularly impressed to see that his little granddaughter was running about in the garden barefoot, like all the other children of Tanzania.

Children are numerous in Africa for various reasons. According to one census in Kenya, families have an average of eight children. One reason is that children are considered as investments. They can help with the farm and home and, when their parents become old, they can look after them. Sadly, so many children die of starvation and illness that the more you have, the more you are likely to see a certain amount survive.

In addition, Africans still retain the traditional belief that after they die there is a possibility they will be born again as a grandchild or great-grandchild. Grandparents worry that too few children will reduce their chances of being reborn.

Health centers in Tanzania are trying to spread the idea of having fewer and healthier children. Yet a nurse told me they first need to educate the people as to why they should have fewer children and what contraceptive methods to use to achieve this.

"We use the pill here," the nurse said. "But the poorer they are, the greater their need. Our supplies of oral contraceptives soon run out and we can no longer continue free distribution. Many of the poor then fall pregnant."

While I was in Tanzania, I visited different kinds of places every day from about six o'clock in the morning to around half past ten at night. The television coverage of my visit tended to concentrate on the children who were starving and the drought, in order to gain public sympathy, but in my capacity as a UNICEF goodwill ambassador, I visited many places that were not shown on television, such as a center for returning the physically handicapped to society; a vocational training center; a cotton factory, where most of the workers were women; a YMCA center for mentally and physically handicapped children; a clinic, a hospital, a juvenile correction center, an orphanage, a slum, numerous elementary schools, a thriving village of healthy and happy families, a village market, various kinds of farms, women's handicraft classes, and bazaars. I also paid courtesy calls on a number of leading government figures. All in all, I must have spent more than one hundred hours being shown a great many different aspects of Tanzania.

Of course, it was not only starving children that I saw, but also many cheerful, happy children: children performing African folk dances and singing impromptu songs most beautifully, children playing on wooden bicycles, which they had made themselves.

And it was in Tanzania that I discovered a most amazing thing.

TANZANIA, 1984

When I was small, I used to be called Totto-chan. That was because Tetsuko sounded to me like Totto, so whenever anyone asked me what my name was, I would reply "Totto-chan!" The title of my book *Totto-chan: The Little Girl at the Window* came about for that reason. And here in Tanzania, wherever I went, each time I visited a place where there were a lot of children, people such as the mayor of the village would invariably shout in a loud voice, "such-and-such *toto*!" or "*toto* so-and-so!" I somehow did not think all these people could have read my *Totto-chan*, but I couldn't help wondering why they kept mentioning my nickname.

When I found out the reason, I looked up to heaven and murmured to myself, dear God, can this be true?

You see, it turned out that the Swahili word for "child" was *toto*, of all things! Wasn't that extraordinary? What a coincidence! To think that the name I was known by as a child should mean "child" in Africa. And to think I heard about it in the first country I visited as I embarked on my work for children.

The word is actually *mtoto* in the singular and *watoto* when it is plural. In Africa, lots of words begin with an *m* or a *wa*, but they are pronounced nasally, so one scarcely hears the *wa*'s and *m*'s. Whenever I have been where people speak Swahili, it has thrilled me to hear anyone calling "*toto!*"

In the original Japanese I called this book *Totto-chan to totto-chan tachi*, which means "Totto-chan and the watotos." It was suggested to me by the illustrator Makoto Wada, who designed the cover of this book.

When the television programs of my visit to Africa were shown in Japan, I worried about what members of the Tanzanian Embassy and other Africans living in Japan would think. There was no doubt that emergency aid was desperately needed, but no one enjoys seeing the underside of their homeland exposed. As a UNICEF goodwill ambassador, my function is to make people aware of the plight of children in developing countries. At the same time, I am supposed to work toward fostering goodwill between our nations.

After the broadcasts, I unexpectedly had an opportunity to meet twenty-five ambassadors from African countries. The Tanzanian ambassador was the first to approach me, and this is what he said:

"When you knelt on the ground in your white dress and held those children in your arms, I was tremendously moved. My eyes filled with tears, and my heart overflowed with gratitude."

I heaved a big sigh of relief.

Jailed for Stealing a T-Shirt

Privation did not necessarily stem from hunger or lack of education.

When I visited a juvenile correction center, twenty or so youths in gray uniforms were lined up for my benefit in the inner courtyard. I wondered what they were in there for, and after the prison guard gave me permission to speak to the children, I asked a boy of about ten what he had done. The boy mumbled that he had stolen a T-shirt.

A T-shirt! The word burst in my ear like a bomb, shocking me.

A T-shirt. Today in Africa almost everyone would like to own a T-shirt because they are in such short supply. No wonder, then, that T-shirt theft is considered such a serious crime. It made me think about how cheap they are in Japan, and how T-shirts are simply given away free to promote and advertise products or events in so many places.

I supposed the boy just wanted to put the T-shirt on and cut a dashing figure.

"Does your father or mother come to visit you here?" I asked.

Scraping the ground with his bare toe, the boy replied, "They've never come, not once."

I imagined it was because his parents had all they could do to cope with their daily tasks. But nevertheless I was sorry for him.

"You won't do it again, will you?" I said, looking him straight in the eye.

"No," he replied, with a rather embarrassed smile.

It was perhaps over and above the call of duty, but I said to him, slowly, "If ever you feel like stealing something again, try and remember that the Japanese lady you met here believes that you have become a good boy and that she is praying for you."

The boy nodded.

The prison guard told me the boy would have to stay in there for another few months. He said there were no boys in the center guilty of murder or any violent crimes.

I can still picture how small those bare feet of his looked in that baggy uniform, as he shamefacedly scraped the earth with his toes. And I cannot help but cry when I think of all the T-shirts that I have been given or bought—T-shirts that I don't wear because I don't think they suit me.

I met many starving children, but my memories are not all sad ones. I had plenty of happy times, too.

There was Mrs. Mongella, a government minister, who went everywhere with me during the whole of my stay in Tanzania. She was a woman of action, but also a very warm person. She was the mother of three boys.

Mrs. Mongella invited the TV crew and myself to a farewell dinner. It was held in the assembly hall of a small elementary school in Dar es Salaam. In her speech, Mrs. Mongella, who had once been an elementary school teacher herself, said, "I could have held this farewell dinner in a hotel or some other more elegant place. But I have read *Totto-chan: The Little Girl at the Window*, and that is why I invited you here. I thought it might remind you of your own elementary school and that you would enjoy eating what the children themselves had cooked. I would not bring anyone else here, as other guests would only think what a poor place I had brought them to, but I thought you would appreciate it."

Mrs. Mongella and I had become as close as sisters. She taught me that no matter what the color of a person's skin, or what language they speak, human beings are alike and can understand one another.

When I left Tanzania, there was a great crowd at the small airport, because the fastest man in Africa, the marathon athlete Juma Ikanga, had just returned from the Olympic Games in Los Angeles. I did not hear what part of Tanzania he came from, but I know that he had been brought up in a disadvantaged community. "Well done!" I thought, mentally clapping with the others, as I bade Tanzania farewell.

Chapter Two

NIGER, 1985

Niger is in the middle of northern Africa, at the southern edge of the Sahara. It covers an area of 489,188 square miles, with a population of about 6.25 million in 1985. It hardly ever rains at all in Niger, and over half of the country has turned into a desert.

The capital is Niamey. I met a Japanese geologist there who was working to help Niger. He told me he had been a classmate of the composer Yasushi Akutagawa through elementary and middle school, and that they used to make music together: Akutagawa on the violin and he on the piano.

"You should play the piano here, like Dr. Schweitzer," I said. He laughed like anything as he replied, "If you brought a piano to this place, it would dry up in no time, and the keys would all drop off!"

I laughed, too, as I pictured the scene, but then, when I thought about the dryness, the cause of this nation's troubles, my laughter stopped short.

Niger means "a great river among great rivers." I read in a book that the Niger River is 2,612 miles long—the third longest river in Africa. It is half a mile wide. Due to the long drought, 97.5 percent of the Niger's majestic waters have completely dried up. It is now a mere 2.5 percent of its former self. This demonstrates how devastating a drought can be.

NIGER, 1985

The Sandstorm

We flew in an army plane the 563 miles from Niamey to Zinder, the country's second largest city. From there we drove in a Toyota Land Cruiser yet another 94 miles to a village called Tanout. We first visited the office of the district governor in Zinder, where there was a large map of Niger. The map had been printed twenty-eight years earlier, in 1957. A small brown patch right at the top of the map—the extreme north of Niger—was all you could see of the Sahara. But by 1985, the year of my visit, more than half of the country had become desert. To think that one half of the entire country could become a desert in twenty-eight years! It was mind-boggling.

Apparently, the Sahara is moving southward at the rate of nine miles a year. It had already reached Tanout, formerly known as the "treasure house of food." The governor explained that Tanout is now on the very front line in the war against desertification.

The BBC correspondent who was traveling with us showed me a publication in English about Niger. It was the first thing written in English that I had seen in Niger, where the official language is French. It was a tourist brochure printed in 1982, just three years before my visit. It said, "It is easy to get to Tanout from Zinder. There is a road that passes through verdant greenery interspersed with thatched dwellings."

The BBC correspondent shrugged his shoulders and opened his palms in the universal gesture signifying, "Well, there is nothing there now!" which was the truth. No road, not a blade of grass, not a single thatched dwelling. Nothing but desert in every direction.

All of a sudden, the governor shouted, "A sandstorm is coming. Get back in the car immediately!"

I looked off into the distance. There wasn't a tree in sight. Not a single building. On the horizon of that arid expanse—even beyond that far-off horizon—I noticed three thin lines of what looked like black smoke. I wondered if they were sand-spouts, but they were obviously miles away, so why the hurry?

I remarked casually to the cameramen, who were busy filming, "I've just been told there's a sandstorm on the way. A sandstorm." I was nonchalant because I had never experienced a sandstorm.

All the while, the governor kept shouting, "Miss Kuroyanagi, come back to the car!" I still could not understand why he was shouting. But I did hurry back into the Toyota.

I was only just in time. The sandstorm, which, beyond the horizon, had seemed to be so far away, had arrived in the space of one or two minutes and had already begun to assault our vehicle. Sand was being hurled against the car and visibility was reduced to zero. We were engulfed in a beige-colored haze. The noise of the sand beating against the windows was deafening. It was like a ferocious blizzard.

Our car set off, following the one in front at a terrific speed. There were two police escort cars in front of us. I wondered why we had to go so lickety-split. The idea was apparently to get out of the sandstorm as quickly as we could. Since it was impossible to see ahead, I wondered how we could avoid running into the car in front at such a speed.

Suddenly, our car swerved off to one side and then proceeded to zigzag through the desert. As the car lurched violently from side to side, I asked the governor why this was happening.

"We have to avoid getting our wheels stuck in the tracks of the car in front," he explained, "because if we do, we'll spin and turn over."

It was indeed like the danger of slipping in snow.

After risking our lives for thirty minutes or so, we finally came out of the sandstorm to find some rain had just fallen. The ground was wet and there were some beautiful puddles. The sky was a brilliant blue, as before. It was the first rain in a year.

"The desert is a strange place," said the governor. "If only it would go on raining for a little longer, in just a week this arid desert would sprout green grass."

Why, the desert must be alive! I thought.

Annual Rainfall: One Inch

In the last year, only one inch of rain fell in Niger. Niger, too, was experiencing a record-breaking drought.

I had no idea how much one inch of rain was. When I was back in Japan, I was listening to a weather report on television. They said,

"Two inches of rain per hour are expected tonight. Precautions are advised." I remembered Niger's *annual* rainfall of one inch and gasped. Tokyo's annual average rainfall for the years 1961–1990 was fifty-five inches.

The governor said to me as we stood in the desert, "Miss Kuroyanagi, can you believe that four years ago there were children here and houses? There were fields. This is what happens when there is no rain."

As I walked around in that area, where everything was now buried in sand, I could see the remains of thatched roofs here and there, proof that people really did once live there. So this is what they meant when they said desertification must not be allowed to come any further. This is what would happen if it did.

It was indeed hot in the desert. "Aren't you hot?" I asked the television crew. "Are you kidding, Miss Kuroyanagi!" was the reply. They showed me the thermometer they had brought from Japan. The red liquid had shot right up to the highest mark of 145 degrees Fahrenheit and burst out of the tube, so now they had nothing with which to tell how hot it was. In Japan, people would start complaining if the temperature was over eighty-six degrees and there was no air conditioning.

Motoring through the desert we came upon the carcass of a cow that had collapsed and died. It had belonged to a tribe of nomads, who had no recourse but to leave it. It had died of starvation, there in the desert where there was neither water nor grass.

The cow had only died a few days earlier, it seems, but the heat had already caused its skin to separate from the bones. Its brown skin looked like an old wrinkled blanket. You could see how tired it must have been from walking, for its hooves were chipped and crumbling. The long black hairs at the end of its tail kept waving in the wind. I felt so sorry for the cow. I wondered what it was gazing at as it died, for its head was pointing to the sky.

Without water, it is the same for human beings. How cruel, I thought. That day I witnessed for the first time the terrors of desertification.

The nomads' cow, dead en route in the desert due to lack of water and grass.

When we were approaching Tanout, we saw our first pond in the desert. Here, some nomad children had brought about thirty goats and sheep to drink. The water was muddy and brown, but the animals were eagerly lapping it up. A boy of about six or seven and two girls were hard at work filling containers with the muddy liquid, for drinking. I could hardly bear to watch.

They were children, but they were working almost as hard as adults. As I have written earlier, children who can go to school are truly blessed; these ones had to find grass and water for their animals, trudging over the desert with their parents all year round.

The three children were from different families, but their animals were all drinking together. I asked the smaller girl if she knew which were her parents' goats and sheep. She replied in the affirmative and told me that each of the animals had names.

"What's that one called?" I asked, pointing to a goat that was just going by. "Gift," she replied immediately.

"Why is it called that?"

"Because someone gave it to us," she replied in her tiny voice, and continued: "Twenty died on our way here."

To lose animals you know by name, who are like members of your family, must be terribly sad, I thought, gazing at her cracked, tough-looking feet, which belied her youthful body.

To these people, the death of their animals means much the same as their own death, for the nomads make a living by traversing the desert, finding grass and water for their animals, then taking them to market to sell when they are full grown.

The goats and sheep were all thin. You could see the bones that formed their ribcages and hips. One of the goats was dying and had fallen to its knees, but still it moved its mouth along the ground hoping to find a blade of grass. From time to time it would find something about half an inch high that looked like withered turf, yet there was so little of it, the goat would get a mouthful of sand as well. I poked about in the sand with my fingers and collected some grass, which I offered to it on the palm of my hand. After the goat had eaten, I thought it seemed a little stronger and its eyes a little brighter. So I collected what grass I could find. It was a strange sort of desert. Seemingly devoid of anything, grass could be found if you scratched about with your fingers, although it looked quite dead. It was as if it were hiding.

The goats' eyes were large and limpid.

The starving children looked just like that goat.

Goodwill Ambassador of Rain

After driving for ages and ages, we arrived in Tanout. As we drove, there had been nothing but desert as far as the eye could see.

The people of Niger had come to the conclusion that this was no time to be praying for rain. "We shall make it rain ourselves," was the cry and, at the line that divided Tanout from the Sahara, the government, with the help of UNICEF, was planting forty thousand trees.

There were no trees in this region and the saplings first had to be grown from seed. The fast-growing acacia was chosen. The seeds were planted one by one in plastic tubes containing soil and watered until they grew to a height of about three feet, after which the acacias were planted out along the dividing line with the desert. This was considered the most effective way to plant as many trees as they could from seed to sapling.

The people from the refugee camps were also helping. There was no underground water there, so wells could not be dug. In order to transplant the acacias, a bucket brigade was organized to bring water from a well about seven and a half miles away. It was more than 145 degrees in the sun.

The acacias were being planted in a line, like a defensive wall on a battlefront. Forty thousand trees, in that vast desert, was like a mere drop in the ocean. But it was better than nothing.

I helped in the turning over of the soil.

Some members of the television crew and some of the journalists who accompanied me were prostrated by the intense heat. There are no trees in the desert for shade. There are no roofs or umbrellas. The ground is so hot that you cannot literally prostrate yourself. To say they just squatted down on their heels and stopped moving would be a more accurate description. For some reason, the heat did not bother me.

Together with the people of Niger, we finally managed to get all the forty thousand saplings planted. All we needed now was rain.

Rain falls on trees and grass, is absorbed by the ground, evaporates and eventually becomes cloud. Later it falls again as rain. Without trees there could be no rain.

We had to get that cycle going. And just then it began to rain! It had rained a little after the sandstorm for the first time in a year. After that, in Niger, I was known as the Goodwill Ambassador of Rain, and they begged me to stay there forever.

They Are Not Being Lazy

When I visited one of the refugee camps in Tanout, I heard a story that moved me deeply. There were usually six thousand people in the camp, yet that day there were only five thousand. I asked why, and was told that, because they heard it had rained in their home villages up north, a thousand of the refugees had rushed home to plant seeds.

The refugees had left the camp to hurry back, barefoot, through the scorching heat, leading their little ones by the hand, all the way to the villages from which they had come—fifty to one hundred miles away. It truly wrung my heart. For after all that, once they planted their seeds, if there was no more rain, the seeds would just be blown away in the next sandstorm. The refugees would then have no recourse but to return to the camp.

In the refugee camp, they could at least get something to eat. To give that up to return to their villages shows the strength of the human spirit. The governor said to me, "In Japan you only need to plant seed once, don't you, to have a harvest? These people must repeat the same work ten or twenty times. So please don't get the idea that Africans are lazy. The effort they put into things is not always something you can easily see. But they never give up hope. And please remember that to give good water to the children is the same as giving them life."

Fleeing from the drought and starvation, people had naturally thronged to the region traditionally known as the "treasure house of food." Tanout's population had subsequently grown from four thousand to twenty thousand people, and the area was no longer in a position to live up to its reputation. In the past six months alone the government—with the help of the Red Cross and other international organizations—had had to create five new refugee camps.

The children in the camps were small and thin, and their skin was often covered with sores. Just before I arrived, several thousand children had died of measles.

Measles is a very serious disease for children. In the 1980s, 2.5 million children a year under the age of five succumbed to the disease worldwide. Even when not fatal, measles is a cause of under-

NIGER, 1985

People waiting in line for food rations at the refugee camp. The temperature was about 120 degrees.

nourishment and pneumonia, diarrhea-induced illnesses, vitamin A deficiency, and handicaps such as loss of eyesight and hearing, which affected about seventy-five million children worldwide. Moreover, it is a disease that can be prevented by inoculation, a standard policy in Japan.

At the refugee camps in Niger, the children's food rations consisted of flour mixed with water, to which a dash of sugar and cooking oil had been added. All they were allowed was one soup-ladle-sized portion of this, morning and evening. That was all. And they were growing children.

The flour was not baked, like bread. There was no firewood. Cooked food was far too much of a luxury for them to hope for. Adults received two ladlefuls, morning and evening, of a slightly thicker mixture, rather like pancake batter. There was no dessert and nothing to drink. Yet, compared with those who were starving, they were far better off.

Wells Provide Life

When we visited one small village, water was gushing from a well 160 feet deep, recently dug by UNICEF. The wells are left to gush for a while before the pump is attached. It was the very first time the children, or indeed the adults, had seen clean, pellucid water. Gathered around the well, the villagers were pouring water over their heads and filling their buckets with the well water.

The children had even begun to dance around the water.

UNICEF had judged that more wells needed to be constructed in Niger to restore the population to previous levels and enable the people to grow their own food as they had in the past. Geologists first survey the land for underground water sources. Arrangements are then made for the necessary technicians and equipment to be dispatched to the locations selected by the geologists. UNICEF invites local people to make tenders for all the necessary manual labor. A number of wells are currently being constructed in this way. Previously, the villagers had to dig wells by hand. Invariably these were shallow, muddy, and yielded little.

The pump is installed after the water has been allowed to flow freely from the well for only one day. A concrete wall—about six and half feet in diameter—is built around the pump, and a fence is also erected to keep out the animals.

Water would not be freely available. The village chief explained that a supervisory committee was to be formed to ration the water to a certain number of pints per family and to arrange for supervision.

I was truly amazed by this. For a tiny village of not more that five hundred people to form a Well Supervisory Committee and make rules—such as no pumping at night—in order to ensure that the well would go on providing water indefinitely, impressed me very much.

The elderly chief said, "Miss UNICEF Goodwill Ambassador, I thank you for this well. Please accept this small gift as a token of our appreciation."

I wondered what I was about to receive, when what should he hand me but three live brown chickens. They were awfully lively chickens, flapping their wings and poking forward their beaks, and I was quite frightened. He had probably kept them carefully for a long time, without eating them, and their legs looked big and strong.

I am very fond of animals but am frightened of chickens because I was chased by some when I was very small. But I thought he would be hurt if I didn't accept them. Concentrating hard on goodwill and smiling, I said, "Thank you very much," and timidly accepted them.

"I won't be able to take these back to Japan," I then said to the governor. "Do you think I could give them to the children of the village to eat?"

The chickens were clucking away, flapping their wings.

"They will be absolutely delighted," replied the governor.

So I said, "Children, I want you all to share these. They are a present for you," and I hurriedly handed the chickens to the leader of the children.

I was deeply touched to have been given those tremendously valuable chickens. All the more when I thought of the governor's words that to give children good water is like giving them life.

I wanted to make people elsewhere understand how wonderful it is to have running water in their houses—pure, clear water they can drink as much of as they want, whenever they want, without it upsetting their stomachs.

What a terrible thing a drought is. To think that the half-mile-wide Niger River had so little water left in it—only a puddle left here and there—that it had become a road that people walked along. Half a mile wide, and you didn't need a bridge because you could walk across the dry river basin. For those of us who are used to four seasons and take rain for granted, you have to see the horror of a drought with your own eyes to understand.

Having no electricity or gas with which to cook their food, the people had cut down all the trees. That is what caused the drought in the first place. Niger's president at the time, Lt.Col. Seynie Kountché, told me they were thinking of buying gas because they couldn't allow any further desertification.

I hope and pray that one day the people of Niger will be able to push the desert back up north, return to their homes, and plant crops.

Chapter Three

INDIA, 1986

"Tetsuko, every year, worldwide, fourteen million children under the age of five die. That is slightly under forty thousand a day; twenty-eight thousand in a week. These figures represent those who die of just ordinary diseases, such as diarrhea and malnutrition. There are now cheap methods of controlling most of these diseases. We at UNICEF want to cut this fourteen million by half by the end of the twentieth century."

That is what James P. Grant, the executive director of UNICEF, said to me with passion when I first met him in his office in New York, in 1984.

Fourteen million! More children were dying yearly than the population of Tokyo. I imagined these were mainly African children, but Mr. Grant went on to say that most of these deaths were actually in Asia. "Though 4.4 million children die each year in Africa," he said, "8.3 million die annually in Asia. Of these, 3.5 million are in India alone, where children die of dehydration from diarrhea and other infectious diseases, all which could be prevented through inoculation. The rest are in Latin America."

The numbers were far greater than I could ever have imagined. And to think that so many children were dying in Asia. I had no idea. Right here in Asia, so close to my own country, 8.3 *million* children were dying annually.

Mr. Grant explained to me how important inoculation was.

I realized then why they had chosen me, an Asian, to be a UNICEF goodwill ambassador. Mr. Grant very much wanted me to go to India.

India is indeed a country with a long history and a beautiful culture, and I was attracted to it for many reasons.

The thing I noticed first on arriving in India was the fact that it was so different from Tanzania and Niger—the countries I had visited earlier—in its beautiful greenery. There was so much verdure everywhere.

India's population in 1986 was 772 million. It was the most populous country in the world, after China.

Tetanus

Following a visit to New Delhi, the capital, I went to Madras, in the south, a city with a population of 4.3 million. Madras is a beautiful town, popular with tourists.

But now, for some reason, ninety-two percent of the children in Madras suffer from malnutrition. Why would ninety-two percent of the children of such a world-famous city suffer from malnutrition? Do only eight percent of the children get enough to eat? It was beyond comprehension.

It was not only in Madras; it is a serious problem facing at least half the children of India. Most of the mothers are undernourished, too, with the result that thirty percent of the children are born underweight. One in every three weighs less than five and a half pounds.

According to government estimates, the income of nearly half of the population is below subsistence level.

The place I was taken first was a children's health center-cum-hospital. It had only been built that year and had about one hundred doctors specializing in treating children with heart, neurological, intestinal and kidney diseases, and blood disorders.

There were two hundred and fifty beds, and they were planning to double that number. Thirty thousand children a year enter the hospital, and an average of twenty-five hundred every day are treated as outpatients. There can't be many hospitals in the world that treat

INDIA, 1986

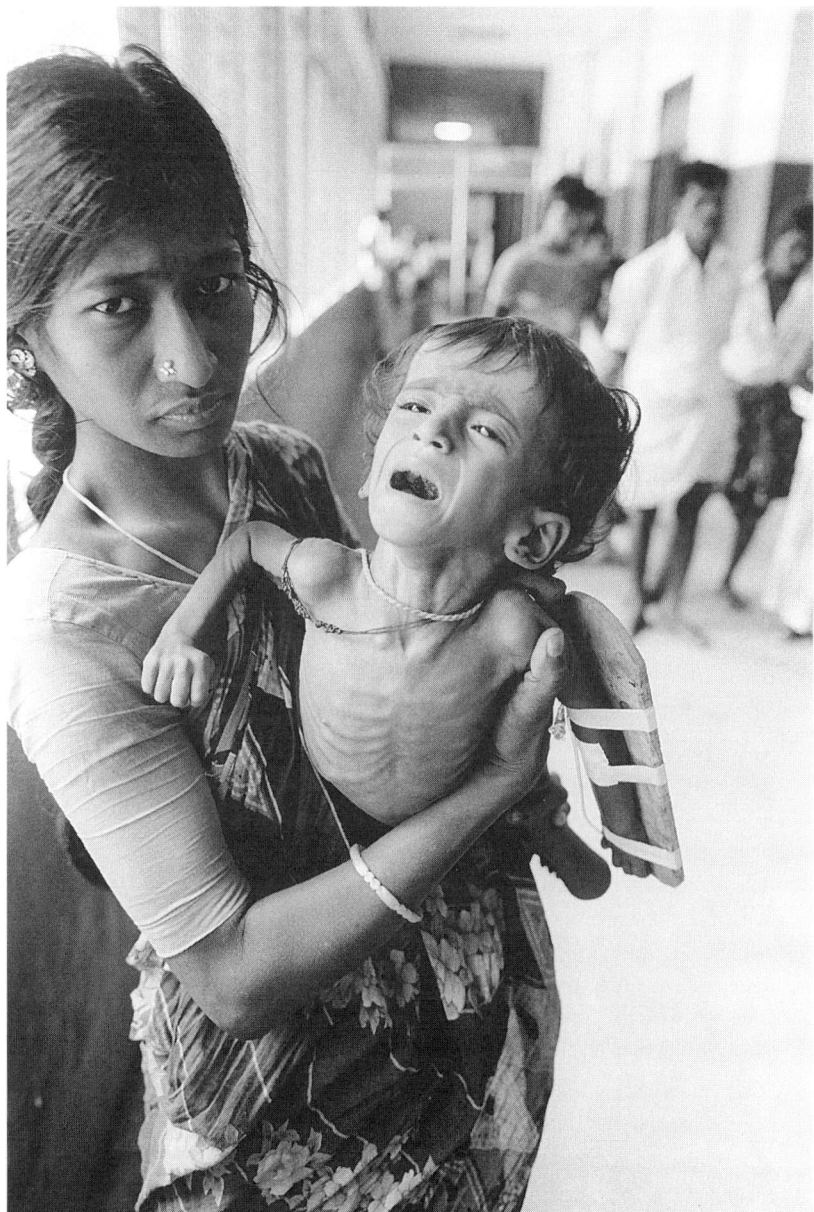

This child has finally been examined. He has dehydration caused by diarrhea and is receiving intravenous fluids. Thus, his spindly arms are strapped to a board.

so many children each day. There was a long, long line of sari-clad mothers who carried babies in their arms or had lain them on the ground as they waited for an examination. Some children among them lay motionless, as if they were already dead, but their mothers nevertheless maintained their place in line, without trying to push ahead and say, "Please, could you see to my child?" In their expressions, it seemed they understood that every mother and every child was in the same dire situation.

A doctor told me that, in India, twenty-four million children are born every year, yet over ten percent of them die within the first year. Forty percent of these deaths occur within the first month, while twenty percent occur within the first week. The main cause of death is tetanus!

Tetanus is caused by a bacterial toxin that affects the central nervous system. Spores live in the soil and cause infection when they are introduced in an injury or wound. The muscles go into a severe spasm. Rigidity develops, which then interferes with breathing. Patients often develop pneumonia, which becomes the direct cause of death. Hygiene has improved so much in my own country that tetanus, an awful disease, is scarcely ever seen there.

About forty years ago, a man I knew who worked as a scene shifter for a TV studio died one day. No one there had ever heard of tetanus; they just thought he had a high fever. By the time it was diagnosed, it was too late. Afterwards it was discovered that the tetanus germ had entered his body through a minor wound. I had seen how quickly the disease runs its course.

In India, homeless children often sleep directly on sewage-soaked ground. Children's ears, apparently, are easily injured. In sleeping on the ground, many get tetanus though ear injuries. Nowadays, however, tetanus is a disease that can be prevented by inoculation.

The doctor of the Madras hospital took me first to a ward with children who were seriously ill with tetanus. There were about fifteen patients in the ward. They were all so thin they looked like dead saplings.

There were so many patients that many of the beds had no mattresses. Some beds just had a thin blanket spread on the iron mesh, upon which the children were lying.

Another aspect of tetanus is that, in addition to rendering the body as thin and stiff as a dead tree, light from the sun or even an electric bulb causes severe muscle spasms in the patient. Thus, curtains were used to keep the ward in partial darkness, though not very effectively.

Neither the doctors nor the nurses seemed to have the time to do anything about a four-inch opening where the curtains had been only loosely drawn together. Sunlight poured through the gap directly onto a patient's bed. The boy in the bed was having muscular seizures. It was heartrending to see that child, thin as a rake, bent double, flailing with his arms and legs. I took some pins from my hair and fastened the curtains together as best I could to keep out the sun's rays.

"I Pray for Your Happiness"

Tiptoeing through the ward to see how the children were, I went and stood beside the bed of a boy at the very end of the row. He looked about ten and gazed up at me with his big, beautiful eyes. The doctor told me the child would recover, but I was afraid this was just said to reassure me, as the boy's condition seemed very bad.

"Feel him," the doctor said, so I touched the child's thin, bony legs. They were hard and dry, and did not feel like human legs at all. That is typical of tetanus. The muscles become stiff and everything rigidifies. He had a fever and was obviously suffering.

He kept looking at me, so I said in Japanese, "The doctor is doing all he can for you, and he says you are going to get well. So cheer up, because everything is going to be all right!"

The child tried hard to say something in reply. I saw then that it was not only his limbs that had become rigid, but everything else, too, including his lips, tongue, vocal chords and jaw. Despite this, that child was trying with all his might and main to say something. I asked the nurse what she thought it was that he had said. The nurse told me that the child, who looked as if he were dying, had said to me, "I pray for your happiness."

I was speechless. I am healthy and have enough to eat. And I

INDIA, 1986

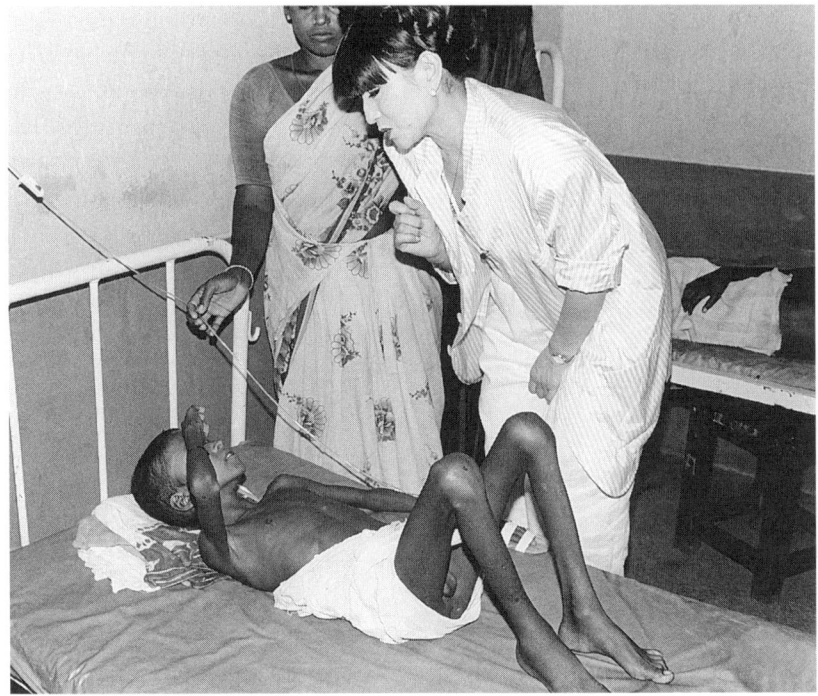

I shall never forget that boy saying to me, "I pray for your happiness."

have had a tetanus shot. Yet that boy at death's door, instead of whimpering or complaining about not having been inoculated, told me he would pray for my happiness. All I could say in reply was, "Please forgive me. I'm terribly sorry I wasn't able to have you inoculated."

The boy's words were quite unexpected.

I was so overcome, I had to leave the ward.

Inoculation!

The next ward was filled with children who were seriously ill with polio.

Near me, a girl of about five was no longer able to focus her eyes.

Her mother stood at her side holding a big black rubber ball. I wondered at first if mother and child were playing with the ball but I thought it odd, considering the child's critical condition. When I looked closer, I saw that the rubber ball had two rubber tubes attached to it, one of which was inserted in one of the child's tiny nostrils. There was no oxygen inhaler available and, since the child could no longer breathe on her own, her mother was pumping air into her lungs with the rubber ball. If she stopped pumping, her child would die.

Without looking at her daughter, the mother went on desperately squeezing the ball with both hands.

I thought about how different it was for children in more technologically advanced countries where proper respiratory apparatuses, with thin tubes, were available for sick children with breathing problems. This little girl had no choice but to have a fat rubber tube forced into her nose and, should her mother's hands stop pumping, to face immediate death.

While I was in the polio ward, here and there I would hear a mother's wail as her child died. It was the same in ward after ward.

All one heard was the wails and screams of the mothers. The children died silently, without a single cry or whimper.

Again, I suddenly recalled the words of that Tanzanian village chief. "Miss Kuroyanagi, it is the children I am sorry for. Adults say so many things as they die—that they are in pain, that they can hardly bear the suffering—but children don't say anything. They simply die silently, under the banana leaves, trusting us adults."

I thought I understood what he meant at the time. But I only understood superficially. It was not until I heard the words of the dying boy, "I pray for your happiness," or saw that small child with the fat rubber tube up her nose, who never uttered any complaint, that I understood what the village chief was talking about.

I stood for some time in the corridor of the hospital, feeling numb.

When I saw the conditions in the hospitals in India, I understood, too, what Mr. Grant, the executive director of UNICEF, had meant when he said, "It is just a matter of inoculation. They must have inoculations!" All those children could have been saved that way.

But you can't have inoculations without refrigerators in which to store the vaccine. There are many children who live in areas without electricity. And even if there is electricity, if it breaks down frequently, the vaccine will perish. Without proper storage and refrigeration, the vaccine will not have the desired effect. Nor will the vaccine be effective if it is old. UNICEF is supporting the development of a vaccine that does not need refrigeration.

Shoelaces

The upper-class women of Madras had set up an active voluntary group called the Women's Volunteer Service of Tamilnadu. The volunteers helped at places like adult education facilities and day nurseries.

I visited one of their facilities—a home for the physically handicapped. There the group ran rehabilitation treatments for victims of leprosy and polio.

The lady volunteers announced, "The UNICEF goodwill ambassador has arrived, and she has brought you some shoes as a gift from the Indian government." The volunteers then proceeded to hand out the shoes, which had been specially designed to help the handicapped walk.

"Now then, put them on, put them on," the ladies said, but the children, who had had polio and were unable to walk without holding onto something, were so unsteady on their limbs that they could not put on the shoes by themselves. Furthermore, shoes and laces were handed out separately, so no one knew quite what to do. The children just held the shoes and laces in their hands, looking puzzled. So I knelt down in front of a child with polio and, after threading the laces into the shoes, put them on her. The shoes had straps right up to the knees. After they were on, the girl managed to walk on her own, using just a cane.

I helped an elderly patient put the shoes on, too, which seemed to make walking so much easier.

A camera crew from India's national television happened to be visiting the home, and they filmed me helping the girl on with her shoes. That scene was shown over and over again on the news. The newspapers carried reports on it for days. The fact that UNICEF Goodwill Ambassador, Tetsuko Kuroyanagi, a celebrity in Japan, had knelt down and tied the shoelaces of a pauper child was news.

I asked what was so amazing about it. The reply was, "Something like that would never happen in India. For an important personage like yourself to assume a position where you would look up at a pauper from below would be unthinkable."

It was I who was surprised. I had obviously heard of the Indian "caste system," and thought that Gandhi had fought against it. Evidently, it still existed.

There was a press conference in New Delhi on the day I was to leave. At the end, a reporter said, "We want somehow to change this country. What do you think we can do?"

I replied, "The fact that you made such a big news story out of what I did, broadcasting it every day, must mean that you thought I did a good thing. So I think things probably are changing little by little. Why don't you try tying a few shoelaces?"

Most of the journalists seemed to welcome fresh ways of looking at things, and the press conference ended on the note of "Yes, certainly we should tie shoelaces."

India's age-old tradition of "caste," or class distinction, is disavowed in the Constitution. Still, in present-day India, in everything from marriage to daily life, severe discrimination is practiced.

In Africa, the site of my previous visit, a great many children were dying from starvation as a result of the drought. Coming to India was a shock to me in quite a different way.

Exotic India, where everyone in the world wants to go! India, with its rich culture, long history and fabulously rich maharajahs. The beauty and refinement of the sari: how often I turned and gazed in wonder at its grace and elegance. During my visit, I learned, too, about the unseen multitude of impoverished children dying of malnutrition.

"I pray for your happiness."

Those words have never left my mind.

Chapter Four

MOZAMBIQUE, 1987

In October, 1987, I visited a country in Africa's southeast, which at the time was said to have the worst conditions in the world, Mozambique.

The population of Mozambique was estimated, in 1987, to be about 14.2 million. Its total area is about 300,000 square miles.

"Mozambique is a beautiful country, I believe, a prime tourist destination," said one of the people who saw me off. It may have been a beautiful tourist destination at one time. It is a rich country; the land is very fertile. And it faces the sea, where many different kinds of fish can be caught. It is world-famous for its prawns. Oranges grow there, too. (I once heard that you can tell whether soil is fertile by whether or not oranges can grow there.) The people of Mozambique are very industrious.

Mozambique had been a Portuguese colony for four hundred years. The natives fought the Portuguese in order to gain independence, a war which cost many lives. In 1975, twelve years before my visit, Mozambique became independent. At that time, only two percent of the people could read. To achieve independence with only two percent literacy is quite something. For the first five or six years, things seemed to have gone well.

The Guerrillas

A successful black administration was a threat to neighboring South Africa, the only country in the world to have instituted a system known as apartheid, a policy of segregation in conjunction with racial discrimination based on color.

Black administrations were already proving successful in the nine countries neighboring South Africa: Angola, Namibia, Botswana, Lesotho, Malawi, Swaziland, Tanzania, Zambia and Zimbabwe.

Conscious of the danger of this, South Africa was supporting antigovernment guerrillas in Mozambique and Angola and supplying them with weapons and money, hoping to bring down black rule there.

Ever since then, the guerrillas have continued to wreak havoc throughout Mozambique. Bridges, railroads, roads, sugar factories and banks have been successively destroyed. Institutions providing health care and education have been particularly hard hit. Between 1982 and 1987, 585 clinics and health centers—half the total number in the country—and over a third of the schools were destroyed.

The guerrillas would always bury land mines in the vicinity of the buildings that they had wrecked. At harvest time, the guerrillas would arrive to plunder the harvested crops, setting fire to the farms, laying waste to everything in sight. They would throw corpses into the wells, rendering the water undrinkable.

Men were killed at random, women were raped and older boys were taken away for use as forced labor and to be trained as guerrillas.

One wondered what happened to the little ones left behind, after seeing their fathers killed before their eyes, their mothers violated and their elder brothers kidnapped. The country was inundated with orphans.

There were many groups made up of nothing but children, hiding in the undergrowth, trying to exist. I met gangs of juveniles who had become unable to rejoin society at large. It was truly tragic.

Combat is always traumatic for the children, since they don't know what it is all about. Having been a child in wartime, I can understand a little of how these young Mozambicans must have felt.

But as an adult coming from peaceful Japan, seeing the tragedy firsthand was a painful experience.

In a hospital that had been destroyed by the guerrillas, a boy lay on the iron mesh of a bed that had no mattress. He was lucky to be able to lie on a bed at all; there are not enough beds to go around. A lot of children were just lying out of doors under the trees.

Some children had lost legs because of land mines. Many had lost an eye due to shrapnel from a bazooka. At the hospital, workers were busy making artificial legs for people who had stepped on land mines. There was a great shortage of doctors, nurses and medical supplies.

Above all, no one knew when the guerrillas would reappear and throw everything into disorder.

As Maputo, the capital, was defended by the army, it was peaceful.

At an agricultural cooperative in the suburbs of Maputo, mothers were working together to study how to grow crops more effectively. I was impressed to see what fine eggplants, cabbages and bananas their farm produced. They were raising pigs, too.

What I thought was really lovely, though, and it was the same wherever I went in Africa—was how these mothers put everything to music and did everything with a song:

> *Come, let's work, let's farm.*
> *Then let's go to the bank.*
> *Come, ladies, let's go out*
> *And work, and go to the bank.*

The women would sing like that, all together, while they worked in the vegetable fields.

Children, too, would start singing at the slightest provocation:

> *Let's overthrow South Africa!*
> *Then we'll all be free.*
> *Stop that old apartheid.*
> *Come on, let's all fight.*

The children at the cooperative seemed quite healthy, yet it pained me to see how their behavior was molded by the prevailing conditions: they were always singing fighting songs, carrying their own handmade wooden guns and assuming poses of belligerence and hatred.

The Necklace

We left Maputo and traveled 435 miles north to Tete Province. To avoid land mines and guerrillas, we separated into several groups and flew there in small aircraft. Instead of airports, we had to land in the "bush." The pilot would get in touch with the military on the ground and have them confirm there were no mines where we were going to land.

The pilots of those small aircraft were volunteers and belonged to a Christian organization called Air Serve. Among them were Germans, Americans, British and Canadians. I was deeply impressed. I thought what a wonderful idea it was to volunteer a skill, such as piloting an aircraft, in the service of a good cause. Here were these experienced pilots, who could have made a good living in a safe country, risking their lives in Mozambique to help fight South Africa's apartheid.

There are no control towers or landing strips in the bush. Nevertheless, these pleasant, attractive men were all very dedicated. I really thought it was wonderful.

Quite unexpectedly, we came across five mothers on the road who had just been rescued from a year's captivity with the guerrillas.

They were practically naked. Their husbands had all been murdered. Three of them were carrying newborn infants, obviously fathered by the guerrillas. The babies were completely naked and were all suffering from diarrhea, their bright yellow feces dripping down the legs of their mothers, who tried desperately to rub it off with their feet so I would not see it.

Some of the women had boys of about eight or nine with them as well—boys who had been used as forced labor. The boys had bald spots on their heads (*alopecia areata*), induced by shock and nervous tension. How sad it was. Mere children, too! What bitter experiences they must have had.

At one refugee camp, there were children trembling, as if with fever, from just such shock: their parents murdered or abused, their houses set on fire, their older brothers and sisters carried away. They had been wandering around all by themselves, trying to escape. What horrendous scenes must haunt their minds. There were children who could not speak, children who had lost their memory, and lots of children suffering from malnutrition and skin diseases.

In 1987, the year I visited Mozambique, the Japanese media reported extensively on a mission to find the relatives of returning displaced children (now adults) who had been left behind in China at the end of World War II. When the war ended, many Japanese, in the turmoil of being repatriated from what was then Manchuria (now northeastern China) were forced by circumstances to leave small children behind. Children who had done nothing wrong! Mothers who could not bear to part from their children!

There were many distraught mothers in Mozambique who had lost their children in much the same way. And there were many children, trying to suppress their tears, who had suddenly become separated from their mothers and were left behind.

One little orphan girl wore a necklace made of seeds, which she said her mother had given her.

"That's precious," I told her. "You may happen to meet your mother one day, and she will be able to recognize you by that, so keep it carefully."

"Yes," said the child, fingering the beads.

One of those war-displaced Japanese wore a good-luck charm she said her mother had put around her neck forty years earlier. She was hoping it would help her find her parents. As I thought of her, it was almost more than I could bear.

A Wonderful Mother

Refugees are often thought of as people who flee to safety across the border of one country into another. In Mozambique, the millions of refugees in camps throughout the country were taking refuge,

MOZAMBIQUE, 1987

There are plenty of brave Mozambican children in the refugee camps.

still within their own country, from the guerrillas.

Since there were so many people in the camps, one might have thought it more logical that they grow their own food rather than depend on rations. Yet, because of the constant threat of guerrilla attacks at the camps and the possible need for their occupants to flee at a moment's notice, growing food was out of the question.

But even in those conditions there were heartwarming stories.

"How many children do you have?" I asked a mother who was breastfeeding her baby.

"Well, let me see. Eight. Oh no, ten!" she replied.

"Can't she count?" I wondered, but that was not the reason. She continued, "I have five of my own, but on the way here, while fleeing from the guerrillas, I saw some children crying because they'd lost their parents. So I brought them along too."

I asked her another question.

"If I were to give you a loaf of bread right now, how many pieces would you divide it into?"

Her reply was immediate.

"Why, ten, of course."

I felt like clapping. In Japan, during the war, I often saw a mother giving hard-to-obtain food to her children, denying herself. It's the natural thing to do. But if a hungry child, who had been separated from its parents, happened to be nearby, the mother would apologize and say, "I'm sorry, but my child is hungry," never sparing any food for the hungry stranger. I could understand the circumstances. But to that mother in Mozambique, it was not "my" children but "our" children—all the children of her country.

That's the kind of people they are. I hoped that soon the civil war would end and that they would be able to live in freedom and with prospects for the future.

Almost like Totto-chan's School

Wherever we went, we wore camouflage and were guarded by soldiers armed with machine guns and bazookas.

One of Africa's biggest power stations is in Mozambique. We went to see it. It is a very large hydroelectric power plant. Its size can be gauged by the fact that only ten percent of the power it can generate is needed to provide electricity for all the people in Mozambique. It could, if needed, provide electricity for the whole of Africa. But the enormous pylons holding the power cables had been toppled over in six hundred places, like dominoes, by the guerrillas. The power lines had been hacked to pieces. As the generators themselves were guarded by the military, they could not destroy those. The turbines inside kept on turning, senselessly, sending the electricity nowhere.

Once the turbines are stopped, it is a serious matter. That is why they were kept going: turning like mad for no immediate purpose whatsoever.

Mozambique has the capacity to produce large quantities of coal. Moatize Station was the railroad station from which the coal used to be shipped. The guerrillas destroyed the railroad, disrupting coal transport. It could not even be mined now. So about one hundred carriages and freight cars stood abandoned, serving as living quarters for about nine thousand refugees, who had fled from the guerrillas. Given that one hundred cars between nine thousand people is not nearly enough, lots of people were sleeping underneath freight cars as well as in open cars.

I was reminded of my autobiographical *Totto-chan: The Little Girl at the Window*. Totto-chan's elementary school was housed in old railroad carriages. When children throughout Japan read the book, they sent me many letters saying things like, "I wish we had classes in a railroad carriage," or "I envy Totto-chan. If they even had just one railroad carriage like that at school I'd like to ride in it," or "It would be like being on a trip all the time, and such fun!"

In the railroad carriages and freight cars at Moatize Station, the children living there had only the clothes they stood up in and ate only what rations they were given. They did not know from day to day what would happen next. Their hair had become light brown from malnutrition, their bellies were distended and they were barefoot. The only water they had to drink was muddy. And, of course, the children could not go to school. Moreover, if the guerrillas ever showed up, they would have to flee again.

MOZAMBIQUE, 1987

I wished I could take a trip with these children in a train like this.

The railroad cars of my elementary school were bright with hope and always filled with laughter, whereas the children in Moatize lived in constant fear. The television crew that had come with me had me get on that stationary train and wave from a window. It seemed a hollow gesture. The children, who had no idea why I was doing that, clambered on board and waved too.

There was something disheartening about being on a motionless train where there was no hope or freedom.

I wondered what Totto-chan's headmaster, who made us those classrooms out of railroad carriages, would have said. He loved children so much, I'm sure he would have been very discouraged. When I wrote that book, I never thought I should one day sit in such a sad train and now, in spite of myself, a tear ran down my cheek.

A girl of about nine with a baby on her back silently wiped the tear away.

Looking at the Future

When I asked the young prime minister if he would give me a message for the Japanese people, he said: "We are combating apartheid, believing that one day it will be gone and we shall all be free. Please tell the people of Japan about us. We'll be happy if they just know something about our country."

At that time, Japan's position was full of inconsistencies. Among the nations trading with South Africa, the only country in the world with a policy of racial segregation, Japan's trade with it was the greatest in volume. We were importing rare metals mined in South Africa and needed in high technology, while South Africa bought goods in exchange. In spite of that, people in Mozambique never once expressed any criticism. I prayed that apartheid would end as soon as possible so that there would be an end to the civil war there.

The day I left Mozambique, I met President Chissano, who had just returned from abroad. I brought him a pair of binoculars, something I was told he did not have.

"Here's something you can use to look for guerrillas," I said.

Beaming, he replied, "No, I shall use them to look at the future!"

I couldn't help envying a country with a president like that.

CHAPTER FIVE

CAMBODIA AND VIETNAM, 1988

ONLY TWELVE YEARS HAD ELAPSED since the unification of North and South Vietnam in 1976, and a mere nine years since the collapse of the terrifying Pol Pot regime in Cambodia in 1979, when I set out on my tour of the region. The foundations of both Vietnam and Cambodia were left in ruins by these two long wars. Most of the people who worked at the hub of their society had been killed. A series of droughts and floods had created a chronic food shortage.

Our visit to Vietnam began in its capital, Hanoi. Before landing in Hanoi, I was stunned to see from the windows of the plane the tremendous number of ponds that had been made by the bombs dropped by American bombers on North Vietnam. The Americans dropped fifteen million tons of explosives, a hundred times more bombs than the number dropped on Japanese soil during the Pacific War. Although twelve years had passed since the end of the war, those ponds—scars left where explosives had blown the earth away—looked from the air like the gaping mouths of hundreds of weird monsters.

Let's Get on with the Reconstruction!

The population of Hanoi was about three million when I was there. It was once known as Little Paris. There were few motorcars on the main street but an abundance of bicycles and rickshaws. I had been told it would be about as cold as in Tokyo, and yet the children were walking about in torn shirts and bare feet. The war, which lasted for forty years, is said to have set the economy back more than twenty years.

The city of Hanoi reminded me of Tokyo right after the end of World War II. Commodities were in short supply, and there was an annual rate of super-inflation of seven hundred to one thousand percent. But no one had nightmares any longer of bombs dropping, and one sensed a freedom from anxiety in people's expressions. Let's get on with the reconstruction! was the prevailing mood.

That said, in 1987, the year before my visit, Vietnam's food supply was severely affected by a drought and a typhoon, as well as a blight and other misfortunes. The harvest was reduced by a million tons. Add to this an annual population increase of one million.

Moreover, the year of my visit, 1988, it had been announced in April that eight million people were suffering from famine, especially in the north, and about three million of them were facing starvation.

I spoke with the foreign minister, Nguyen Co Trach Tak, for about an hour and a half. He was a charming man, and he opened his heart to me.

He said, "We realize that the romantic revolution we had in mind was a failure. We now want to become friends with all the nations of the world."

What he meant was, Vietnam's economic policy was a failure and the country was bankrupt.

The marketplace in Hanoi bustled with people. There were a great many varieties of vegetables. Eggplants were five hundred dong, or the equivalent of about a quarter, a kilo. Bean curd was only a dime a slab. Food staples seemed cheap. A chicken, however, was two thousand dong (about one dollar). That seemed cheap enough compared to Japanese prices, but the average monthly salary of a Vietnamese civil servant was only thirty thousand dong (about fifteen dollars), which made the two-thousand-dong chicken an expensive luxury.

Beauty salons displayed photographs of the latest hair styles. Hanoi was livelier than we imagined it would be when we looked down on it from the airplane. Everyone was pitching in. Reconstruction seemed to be in full swing.

The children all looked trim and attractive. I could see why Vietnamese children are said to be cute.

The Scars of Cambodia

We left Hanoi and set off by plane for Phnom Penh, the capital of neighboring Cambodia. From the air, Cambodia was lush and green as far as the eye could see. About seventy-three percent of the country is covered by forest, and the country should have been untouched by hunger and starvation. However, war and genocide have left the country deeply scarred.

Over a million people are believed to have been massacred during the three years and eight months of Khmer Rouge misrule that began in 1976, a year after Pol Pot and his supporters seized control of the Cambodian government. No one will ever know for sure exactly how many people were killed. One government official told me that the death toll was probably closer to three million. The Khmer Rouge first moved against the most influential people of the old regime. They killed scholars, teachers, doctors, top government officials, priests and actors. They even recalled those who were studying abroad and killed them, too. It is frightening enough just to think about. It is said that within the intellectual class, eight out of every ten people were murdered. The film *The Killing Fields* is a very accurate portrayal of Cambodia under the Pol Pot regime.

By 1986 Cambodia's population was badly unbalanced: of the approximately 7.5 million inhabitants, sixty-four percent were female and thirty-six percent male.

That was not all. The Pol Pot regime forced several million people to move from their homes, leaving ghost towns. Families and married couples were separated. People were forced into farming cadres, and money and trade were abolished, throwing the economy into chaos. Doctors' instruments for performing operations, dentists' equipment, everything was destroyed. The school system, too, was abolished. The regime wanted to annihilate the existing culture and civilization. It seemed bent on destroying the people and the nation.

Nine Thousand Skulls

We visited the Tuol Sleng Museum, the notorious detention center once under the direct control of the Pol Pot regime. Originally a middle school, Pol Pot's security forces took it over and turned it into a prison and torture center. Of the 14,500 people known to have been put to death there, 2,000 were children.

Barbed wire had been stretched around the windows on all three floors of the building to stop people from jumping to their deaths. There was a crazy rule regarding torture: no one was permitted to make a sound. No matter how much it hurt, how much they wanted to cry out, the tortured must keep silent. These were the circumstances in which the massacres took place every day for almost four years.

The museum walls were covered with photographs of the victims, taken just before they were killed on the day of their "release." There were still bloodstains on the floor of the torture room. We were shown the bed where the prisoners had been shackled by the wrists and ankles. And we saw the desk that had been used during interrogations. Many people were tortured at Tuol Sleng before being executed.

Instruments of torture that had been preserved included a long iron rod, from which prisoners would be hung upside down, their hands tied behind their backs; and an enormous pot, which would be filled with water, and into which the victims would be dunked, head first, until they drowned.

I had heard the Pol Pot faction had massacred over a million people. But to stand in the very same room where the victims had actually been tortured, and see the tiny compartments into which they had been thrown, heavily shackled, sent cold shivers down my spine.

The photographs, which covered a whole wall, were of the people who had been slaughtered. I had been told that children had not

CAMBODIA AND VIETNAM, 1988

"What's going to become of our children?" those skulls seemed to be crying out, weeping.

been killed, but there were many children among those photographed. There were kids of elementary school age as well as middle school age. This place had once been a school. I wondered what they thought as they were brought here.

I remembered hearing about Pol Pot, but I had no idea that what he had perpetrated was as cruel as this. Was there really nothing we could have done about it?

As I stood there, on the site of what had once been a school, I seemed to hear the echo of happy voices and laughter. But these children were forbidden to cry or shout or laugh.

"I pray that it will never happen again."

That is what I wrote in the visitors' book.

The sites of massacres throughout Cambodia had been left just as they were.

At the Choeung Ek mass grave on the outskirts of Phnom Penh, twenty thousand people had been killed.

I stood in the midst of nine thousand skulls. They were still unearthing skulls there, and some were in the process of being cleaned. They were being soaked in water-filled pots to loosen the dirt, then piled up on the grass, with their mouths gaping.

"Why did I have to be killed?" "What's going to become of our children?" That's what those who were murdered seemed to be crying out, weeping.

It was quiet on that grassy plain. The large holes here and there were ones the prisoners had been forced to dig before they were killed. As soon as the holes had been dug, the prisoners had their hands tied behind their backs and were made to kneel at the edge of the hole. As they knelt, their skulls were cracked open with axes. They were then kicked into the hole, and the hole was filled in. In the years that followed the Pol Pot regime, the collective graves became thickly wooded. In this area alone, 129 holes were found, of which 86 had been excavated. Half of those massacred still lie buried.

It was the first time I had ever seen a real skull, let alone nine thousand. I had always found imitation ones scary enough. Looking at those nine thousand skulls wasn't scary at all, or even unpleasant.

I just felt terribly empty. And I seemed to hear the voices of those who were killed weeping and grieving for their country.

An Old Man's Hands

During the days of the Pol Pot regime, the eight hundred-some hospitals throughout the country were all destroyed.

In Phnom Penh, Cambodia's only national children's hospital was rebuilt from its ruins. There were 150 beds, and outpatients numbered 500 to 600 daily. Yet there were only 14 doctors and 157 other staff members, including nurses.

The director was to have been killed, but he looked so thin that Pol Pot's soldiers mistook him for a peasant. Since he did in fact come from a farming village, he was able to get away with his life by taking refuge in the paddies, planting rice.

With tears in his eyes, the director told me, "Out of the five hundred doctors in Phnom Penh, only thirty-two of us survived. My classmates were all killed. As for the dentists, only one is still alive."

Alongside the hospital beds with small children in them, worried-looking mothers remained standing. Medicines were in such short supply, there was little that could be done for patients except to watch over them. The corridor floors were overflowing with children for whom there was no room in the wards.

Infant mortality in Cambodia is very high. One in every five children under five dies. Most die of malaria, followed by tuberculosis. I was told that ten percent of the TB patients were under fifteen.

We visited the National Tuberculosis Institute. In the pulmonary tuberculosis ward for children, the young patients were sitting up in bed, holding pieces of cotton cloth over their mouths "so as not to infect other people," according to the doctor's instructions.

"I don't mind," I said. "They're nice-looking, and I want to see their faces." All the boys lowered their hands and the cloths they were holding, and smiled. Their smiling faces were beautiful. But when I shook hands with them, I noticed that their hands were as thin and shriveled as an old man's.

More children were lying on the floor under the beds and in the narrow passageways in between. It was hard to believe, but the children lying on the floor were apparently those not expected to recover. I was astonished to see seriously ill patients lying on the floor. In most countries, priority is given to the patients who are the most ill. But in a country that is in tight circumstances, priority is given to treating those who have a good chance of recovery.

I met the welfare minister. He said, "We are very poor indeed. What we need most now is medicines for children. We have nothing."

How Beautifully Dressed You Are!

The scars left by massacres and fighting during the Pol Pot regime can be witnessed in many forms.

For one thing, the regime left about three hundred thousand orphans. Scarcely one percent of them are in orphanages, of which there are only thirty-five in the whole country. The children in the orphanages are lucky. All the children you see walking about in the town are barefoot.

I visited a country orphanage for small children. Seeing that the infants were aged from about eighteen months to three years old, I offered one little boy a piggyback ride. He didn't seem to have ever ridden piggyback before and laughed with glee. It made me laugh, too, and when I looked behind me, what should I see but all twenty of the children lined up waiting their turn for a ride. All well behaved, patiently in line! I warmed to the spirit of the occasion and gave them piggyback rides, one after another. There were some who did not know what to do and, instead of clinging to my back, sat on it as if they were riding a horse. So, finally, I crawled on the floor like a horse while the children sat on my back. I went on doing this for ages but never seemed to come to the end of the children. I found that they were all lining up again for second rides! I would say, "Hey, haven't you already had a ride?" but the child would just grin sheepishly and then go and join the end of the line.

All the orphanages were very short-staffed. No one knew how long the children had been separated from their parents, but each child seemed to long for someone to care for them. This is why I

CAMBODIA AND VIETNAM, 1988

It started with a piggyback ride. Soon all the children wanted to have a turn and I ended up on my hands and knees, letting them ride me like a horse.

went on giving piggyback rides until well after dark, while the TV cameramen pleaded with me to be careful and not slip a disk.

The children were all beautifully dressed. It wasn't until the following day that we discovered the clothes had all been specially rented or borrowed for our visit.

Takeyoshi Tanuma, the photographer who always accompanied me on these visits, had been taking pictures of me giving piggyback rides. When we got back to our lodgings that night, Tanuma, who is a world-famous photographer, told me he was not satisfied with the pictures, having had to use a flash on account of the fading light.

"I'd like to take some piggyback pictures again, tomorrow morning," he said, "without a flash."

The UNICEF people agreed and said they would get in touch with the orphanage. But the director, who had welcomed us so warmly the day before, flatly refused.

"It wouldn't be convenient," she said, then added, "Please come in the afternoon."

That's when we learned the reason for her refusal. Apparently the children had nothing to wear and went naked most of the time. When they heard I was coming to visit, the administration had obtained clothes for all the children to wear. "I don't mind," said Tanuma. "They would look sweet with nothing on!" But the director was adamant. "No," she said. "That wouldn't be fair on the children. Please wait and come this afternoon."

After that, I visited many orphanages in many countries, and it was the same everywhere. There would be children hurriedly fitted out with shoes far too large for them or children in baggy clothes that didn't fit at all. So whenever I saw children who were beautifully dressed at orphanages, or sometimes even at elementary schools, it always disturbed me. I could understand the teachers' feelings, yet at the same time the children looked so unnatural in clothes they were not used to wearing and which were probably ill fitting and uncomfortable.

I did appreciate the teachers' efforts to receive me, the goodwill ambassador, with everything as nicely presented as possible. I wanted to express my thanks—although I wasn't really all that grateful—so I always made a point of saying to the children, "Oh, how beautifully dressed you are!" The teachers would beam with pleasure.

During the war, I had only one dress. As I grew, it got so I could hardly get into it. I outgrew my shoes, too, and a pair of wooden clogs given to me by a kind lady became my only footwear while we were evacuated. In the winter, I went to school in straw boots. I remember how cold my feet were with the snow that soaked through the straw. It was the same for everybody then. Now I have to have a great many dresses and shoes for my work. Still, I was glad for those early experiences, which enabled me to understand a little how the teachers felt.

That afternoon when we returned, the children of the orphanage were all dressed in their lovely clothes. I gave them piggyback rides and pretended to be a horse, and the children had a wonderful time.

Even at the orphanages, there was no powdered milk or anything nourishing for the children to eat. A major problem there was that the nurses themselves were orphans, so they did not know how infants should be treated. None of this was the children's fault.

Many of the children from orphanages have now been adopted. The year before I was there, twenty children from the orphanage I visited had been found homes. Foster parents included Cambodia's prime minister.

The Only Actor Who Survived

There were some young men and women who were trying to revive ancient Khmer music and traditional dances, which had almost been annihilated during the Pol Pot era. Over ninety percent of these young people were orphans whose parents and siblings had been killed.

The minister of culture, who explained these ancient arts to me, was a big, warm, mild-mannered man. He said, "Miss Kuroyanagi, you are an actress, I believe. I, too, am an actor, the only one who survived."

I was nonplussed. There usually has to be more than one actor to put on a play, so he would not have been able to act anymore. He would not even have had anyone with whom to talk about theater. He was probably a good actor, too. How lonely he must have felt with all his colleagues killed, left only with their memories. Being in the theater myself, I could well understand the deep sorrow I sensed in his gentle face.

Almost all the elementary school teachers were killed, too. A shortage of teachers necessarily means a reduction in the quality of education, one of the country's greatest challenges. Nevertheless, the minister of culture told me that since priority had been given to children's education and the reeducation of adults, Cambodia's literacy rate was now actually very high.

Besides the shortage of teachers, elementary schools also face a shortage of teaching materials. At one elementary school I visited in a Phnom Penh suburb, five pupils had to share one textbook. Many elementary schools in the country can only provide textbooks for the teachers and cannot afford blackboards, desks, chairs, notebooks, pencils, paper and ink. Classrooms are scarce, too. No wonder over one hundred pupils had to wait at least a year to attend the school I visited.

Only three percent of the water is safe to drink in the whole of Cambodia. Even in the cities, only about ten percent is potable. UNICEF continues with its aim to dig one well for every two hundred people in the country.

Angkor Wat

At the end of our visit to Cambodia, we were invited to go to Angkor Wat, the nation's symbol and one of the mysteries of the Far East. "You must at least see what remains of our heritage," said the government, as they arranged for us to go. While the war in Cambodia raged on, the rest of the world worried as to what would become of this great stone masterpiece.

Angkor Wat is 160 miles northwest of Phnom Penh. We flew there with a military escort.

The road to Angkor Wat, a twelfth-century temple in the middle of dense jungle, is long and straight and goes on and on.

The first-class hotels that once stood in a row facing Angkor Wat were all destroyed by the Pol Pot faction, without leaving a trace. Pol Pot's people had also knocked off almost all the heads of the stone statues that stood in rows inside. Had they carried them away? The stone statues stood there, headless, side by side. Restoration is under consideration, though the artisans capable of the work have all been killed and little, therefore, can be done. From time to time, artisans from India have come to collaborate on the work.

Empty ammunition cartridges lay about everywhere on the grounds. They looked so out of place in beautiful Angkor Wat.

Occasionally, far off in the distance, we could hear the boom of shells fired by soldiers of the Pol Pot faction. Otherwise, the only sound was that of insects. It was so quiet it was hard to believe there had been a long war. I hoped that peace would soon come to this country so that Angkor Wat and Angkor Thom, both masterpieces of the former Khmer empire, could be visited freely by everyone.

My visit to Cambodia was nearing its end. But everything I saw was overlaid in my mind by that vision of nine thousand skulls piled high, looking up at the sky.

The minister of education and the welfare minister gave a dinner in my honor at which music was provided by a five-man band, which played "Sukiyaki" specially for my benefit. You could see they were hoping I would be pleased. When I stood up and clapped, they smiled. But actually, the piece made me sad. It was the first time I had heard "Sukiyaki" played anywhere abroad since my very good friend Kyu Sakamoto, the singer, had died the previous summer. The piece made me sadder than it ever had, played there in that dimly lit room.

Vietnam's Night Elementary School

We left Phnom Penh at 6:00 A.M., driving overland, once again, on National Highway 1 bound for Vietnam. It was a ten-hour journey by car. After we had gone about an hour and fifteen minutes, we arrived at the Mekong River crossing. The Mekong River is astoundingly wide and brimming with water.

At the crossing we embarked on a ferry. When it reached the opposite bank, we were in Vietnam. The ferry was crowded with people carrying loads on their heads. Some had birds with them, others had livestock.

A girl of about ten, with curlers in her hair, was selling some kind of food that looked like spring rolls, a specialty of Vietnam. It was the time of day when a girl of that age would normally be in school. Alas, no one bought any spring rolls, and it looked as if she would not do much business that day. Other children were selling vegetables and fruit. They were all working instead of going to school. Supposedly, fifty percent of the children enrolled in elementary school in Vietnam drop out because they have to work.

After crossing the Mekong by ferry, we continued our ten-hour drive by car along National Highway 1, through what seemed to be mostly wasteland, to Ho Chi Minh City (formerly called Saigon, the capital of South Vietnam). With a population of four million, Ho Chi Minh City is Vietnam's largest city. It goes without saying that this town, too, was suffering from the aftereffects of war. Compared to Hanoi, it was lively, yet, within the city, there were eighty thousand vagrant children, seventy thousand prostitutes and an unknown number of drug addicts, all figures attesting to the tragedy of the situation. Fifty percent of children under five suffered from malnutrition.

The mayor and lady deputy mayor of Ho Chi Minh City, both of whom I met, were of the same opinion as the foreign minister whose acquaintance I had made in Hanoi.

"Unless the economy improves, we can't go on," they said. "There are all sorts of bad habits left over from the old days, but one thing we must change at the very least is the elementary schools, which should be turned into daytime schools instead of the night schools that we have now."

The deputy mayor said it upset her terribly.

There were about a million school-age children in the city. Of these, about sixty thousand either bravely went to work each day to contribute to the household economy, looked after their younger siblings or helped with the housework and, therefore, could not attend elementary school in the daytime. The night elementary schools were for their benefit.

We visited one of these night schools. It was called the Kim Lien Pagoda School. It was in a particularly poor district of Ho Chi Minh City and was housed in a small nunnery that had been lent for the purpose. It was open from 7:00 P.M. to 9:30 P.M. There were seven teachers and 193 pupils, ranging in age from six to fifteen. It was the first time I had ever seen a night elementary school. There were none in Africa, India or Cambodia, the places I had visited thus far.

Small children about six years old were rubbing their eyes in the dim electric light as they did their lessons in reading and arithmetic out loud in their sweet little voices. Some of the children's eyes kept closing. They had to prop them open with their thumbs and forefingers.

The biggest problem was the extreme shortage of notebooks, textbooks and stationery. As there wasn't even sufficient paper and pencils, the children were writing with tiny letters on yellowish

CAMBODIA AND VIETNAM, 1988

A night elementary school. Children as young as this work in the daytime, like adults, and come here at night.

paper made from straw. They had to keep their writing tiny in order to save paper. It's hard for children in their first years of school to write so small. Yet all their letters looked like little ants. I thought with shame how big my own handwriting was, and how I thought nothing of tearing up sheet after sheet of paper. A lot of the children were using pen and ink because they had no pencils.

Many of the pupils were war babies—mixed-blood children, the products of liaisons between American soldiers and Vietnamese women.

The teachers, too, kept saying that they hoped the economy would improve so that all these children would be able to go to school in the daytime instead of at night—these children who were so poor they had to use the daytime to work and were only free to do their lessons in the evening.

As I watched a little boy of about six reading from the blackboard in his innocent, artless voice, I suddenly began to cry. A boy of six in Japan would be in the first year of elementary school. His parents would have bought him a satchel. He would check the next day's schedule to see when he could watch TV, when he would have his bath and when he would go to bed. There is no doubt that Japanese children have to study hard; they sometimes even have to go to "cram" school to be able to assimilate it all. But I think they are happier than these children. I am only sorry to think that our children don't realize how fortunate they are. This was the reason for my tears.

It Is the Children Who Suffer the Most

The defoliant used by the Americans during the Vietnam War, the unexploded bombs that suddenly go off, and such things as malnutrition, are all responsible for the five thousand blind children who live in Ho Chi Minh City. At the time of my visit, there were not many schools for handicapped children.

Nguyen Dinh Chien School for blind children had eighty-one pupils from all over Vietnam. The students were all boarders. As in the other schools, they did not have enough supplies and stationery

CAMBODIA AND VIETNAM, 1988

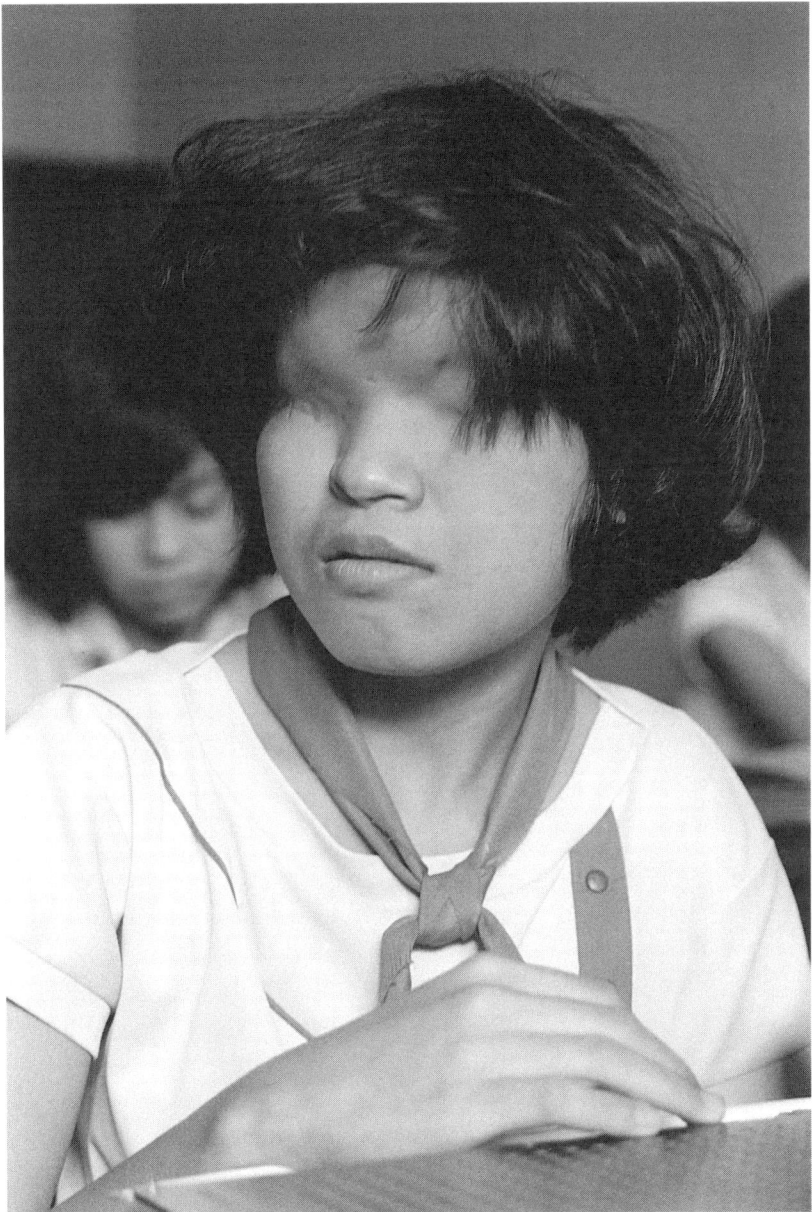

The girl who was born with no eyes—an effect of defoliant—held up her bangs and showed me her face.

to go around. The only aid from abroad had come from the Dutch, who had made it possible for the school to have textbooks in Braille.

There was a ten-year-old girl who had lost her left arm and both eyes when an unexploded bomb went off. She had glass eyes, but she was pretty and clever. She read to me as she fingered a Braille text. Because of poverty, children frequently sustain such injuries when helping their parents till the fields, where unexploded bombs often go off. It is heartbreaking when one realizes that nothing is being done to prevent future accidents like this.

There was a girl who had been born with no eyes at all, a nasty side-effect of the defoliant. About middle-school age, she wore her hair in bangs that covered her forehead. When I said, in Japanese, "*Konnichi wa?*" ("How do you do?") she greeted me back in Vietnamese.

The teacher asked her to push back her hair. She held it up so I could see her face. The skin was a smooth expanse from brow to cheek, covering her eye sockets. I heard the TV cameraman behind me gasp. Her face was like a death mask, blank and expressionless. The teacher must have encouraged her to wear bangs so as not to shock people. But when I squeezed her hand, the child's mouth broadened into a lovely smile.

"Keep smiling!" I said, as I left the room. When I looked back, I saw her desperately pulling down her bangs again to hide her face. That child will go through life like that, hiding her face, I thought. That blameless, innocent child.

I could scarcely bear it. There she was, studying her Braille without so much as a complaint. Here, too, I couldn't help thinking that it is the children and the mothers who suffer most.

The blind school children put on a performance for us. There was a boy playing the guitar with superb style, although he had never in his life seen anyone playing the guitar.

Viet and Duc

The defoliant used by the Americans was still wreaking havoc. I visited the Tu Du obstetrics and gynecology hospital, where the

Siamese twins Viet and Duc were. With a pathetic expression on her face, the lady director told me that an average of five deformed babies a week were being born there. Ten sets of Siamese twins had been born at the hospital the previous year. Viet and Duc have been separated, but the others will have to remain attached for the rest of their lives. Because of the mothers' malnutrition, one in every five newborn babies weighs less than five pounds.

The only good news was that Viet and Duc were flourishing. It was two months since they had been separated, and Duc was already well enough to whiz around the hospital corridors in a wheelchair. Viet was still confined to his bed, but his reactions had improved, and he was able to shed tears. They said he had also gained six pounds and six ounces. "Get well soon!" I said, giving the two boys a panda hand puppet and a stuffed toy cat that moved, too. Though they said Viet's reactions were slow, he broke into a smile as I made the panda move.

I asked cheerful, energetic Duc to do me a favor. When he had finished his studies and become independent, and could travel around the world, I said I wanted him to tell people what happened to him. If he could explain how he was affected by modern technology, he could make people aware that there must be peace and freedom. I said I wanted him to be an envoy of peace. Duc clearly replied that he would.

There are bound to be hardships aplenty. Nevertheless, Vietnam and Cambodia were determined to resurrect their countries and filled with optimism for the future. It is wonderful to see people so proud of their country. I am so glad I went there.

CAMBODIA AND VIETNAM, 1988

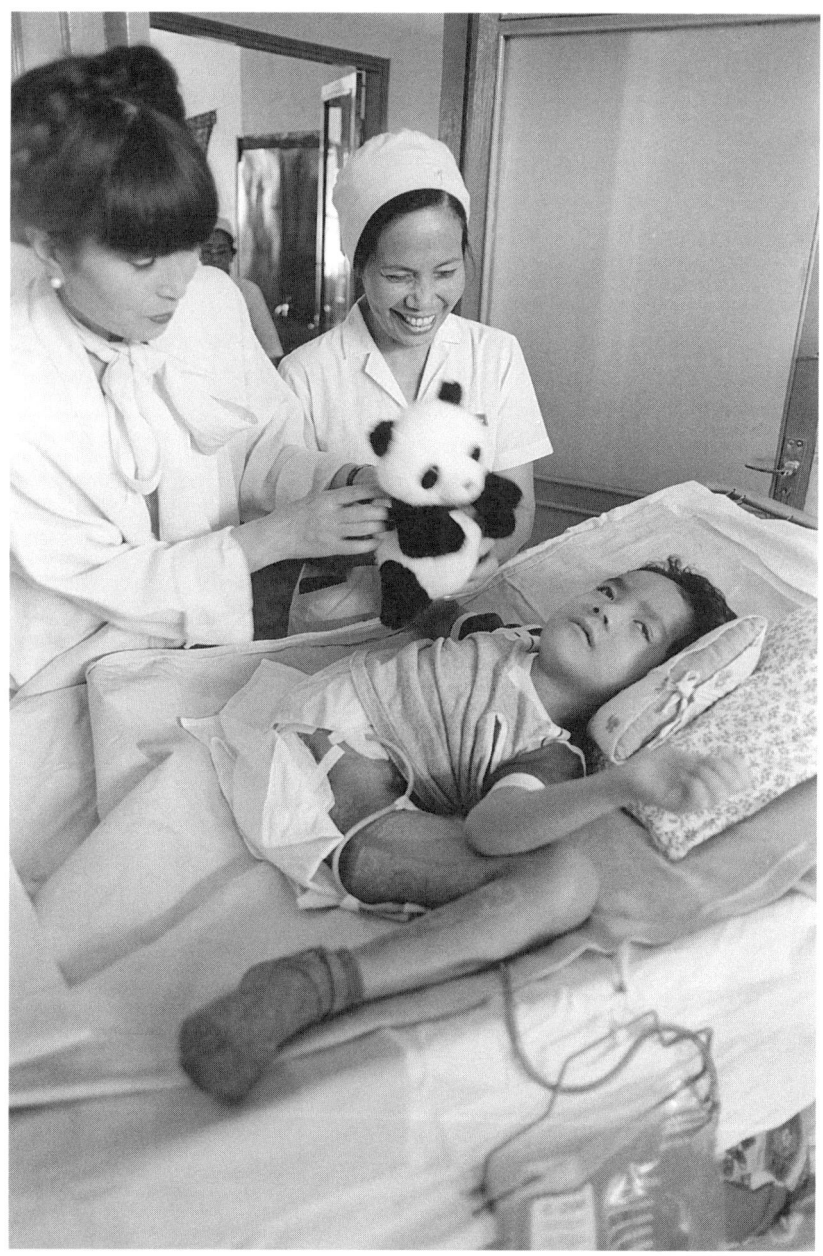

Even Viet, who was in a poorly state, smiled when I showed him the panda.

CHAPTER SIX

ANGOLA, 1989

AS SOON AS IT IS DECIDED WHERE I will be going next in my capacity as UNICEF goodwill ambassador, I start finding out about my latest destination. I ask people who have lived and worked in the country —correspondents and journalists, people sent there by the welfare ministry and foreign office and, sometimes, ambassadors—to spare me as much time as they can to tell me about its government, its economy, its customs and its religion.

Angola is just north of South Africa, off to the west, facing the Atlantic Ocean. The population in 1989 was about ten million. Its capital is Luanda, and the official language is Portuguese. Formerly rich in natural resources such as diamonds and iron ore, it is a country that would have no problems in peacetime. There is also oil and gold. Rare metals needed in high technology can be mined there, too.

The predominantly Portuguese engineers and technicians, however, all left when Angola won its independence. The remaining Angolan technicians were few in number because most Angolans had only been employed as laborers. Moreover, the farmers were conscripted to form an army to protect the newly independent country, a policy that reduced food production. Production of its renowned coffee dropped to about one tenth of what it was at its zenith. Angola now found itself in a situation where sixty percent of its budget had to be put aside for defense. Civil war had been going on for such a long time, it was said that out of a thousand children, 375 died before reaching the age of five.

The Official Guest House

At the end of October 1989, after learning much about the country, I set off for Angola.

The first thing I saw on arriving in the capital, was countless soldiers on crutches. Their legs had been blown off by land mines.

Angola differed from the other countries I had visited mostly in that civil war had been going on there for fifteen years. If you added to that their fourteen-year struggle for independence from Portugal, it meant that the Angolans had been at war for nearly thirty years. Thirty years of fighting! It was beyond the limits of my imagination. There were no proper buildings left standing. The glass was broken in most windows.

The official guest house, where I stayed, was built in the Portuguese style. The electricity was forever breaking down. When I think about it, the places I stayed in Niger, Mozambique and Vietnam were also called "official guest houses," which may sound very grand, but after visiting places all day, when I came back at night and wanted to wash my feet in the bathroom, most of the time there was often no water—let alone hot water—in the taps.

In my bedroom in the official guest house in Mozambique, I spied an eight-inch spider crawling across the ceiling. It was pure white with black stripes—a most fearsome-looking spider. I was terrified that it might drop down onto my face. After a tremendous scuffle with a can of insecticide spray, I managed to exterminate it. I'm not fond of large spiders in Japan, but I suppose I'm resigned to them or something, because they don't scare me all that much. Here, I was terrified of finding one in a shoe or my clothes. So I made a point of putting all my clothes back into my suitcases at night and fastening the zippers. It was a lot of trouble, but there you are!

When I told them I wanted to wash my feet at the official guest house, several small buckets of water were brought to me and poured into the bathtub. When the water had settled, there was two inches of muddy sediment at the bottom of the tub. If that was what it was like at the official guest house, I could only imagine how much worse the water must have been elsewhere, not to mention the water used for drinking.

Bringing Your Own Seat to School

Angola reminded me of Mozambique when I visited it two years earlier, in 1987.

Mozambique had won its independence from Portugal twelve years before that and had managed well at first. Shortly thereafter, neighboring South Africa, which considered successful black rule a threat, began to support the antigovernment guerrillas and to supply them with weapons and money. The guerrillas proceeded to wreck the whole country, destroying hospitals and schools and hacking the railroad to pieces. Refugees fleeing from the guerrillas were huddled in camps of several thousands in some places and millions in others. Refugees in their own country!

But it was even worse in Angola.

One morning I noticed some children walking along with strange little wooden contraptions on their heads. I wondered what it was they were carrying, and discovered they were taking their own seats with them to school. They had no satchels with them, nor lunch boxes, only stools for sitting on. They were all barefoot.

Some of you may think Africans walk barefoot because of the heat. In fact, those who do not wear shoes do so because they have none. It hurts to walk barefoot over rough ground. Any child who owns footwear wears it. But, in Angola, I seldom saw a child who did.

Schools as well as orphanages in Angola had no desks or chairs. The children sat on the bare concrete floor, although kids who were better off would bring a small stool from home. The stools looked as if they were made of odd scraps of wood, for there was a drought, and wood was scarce. The schools and orphanages had no money to buy chairs. Nor were there any shops from which to buy them even if they had had the money. All the shops were closed because of the long civil war. There was nothing to sell. It was like that during

ANGOLA, 1989

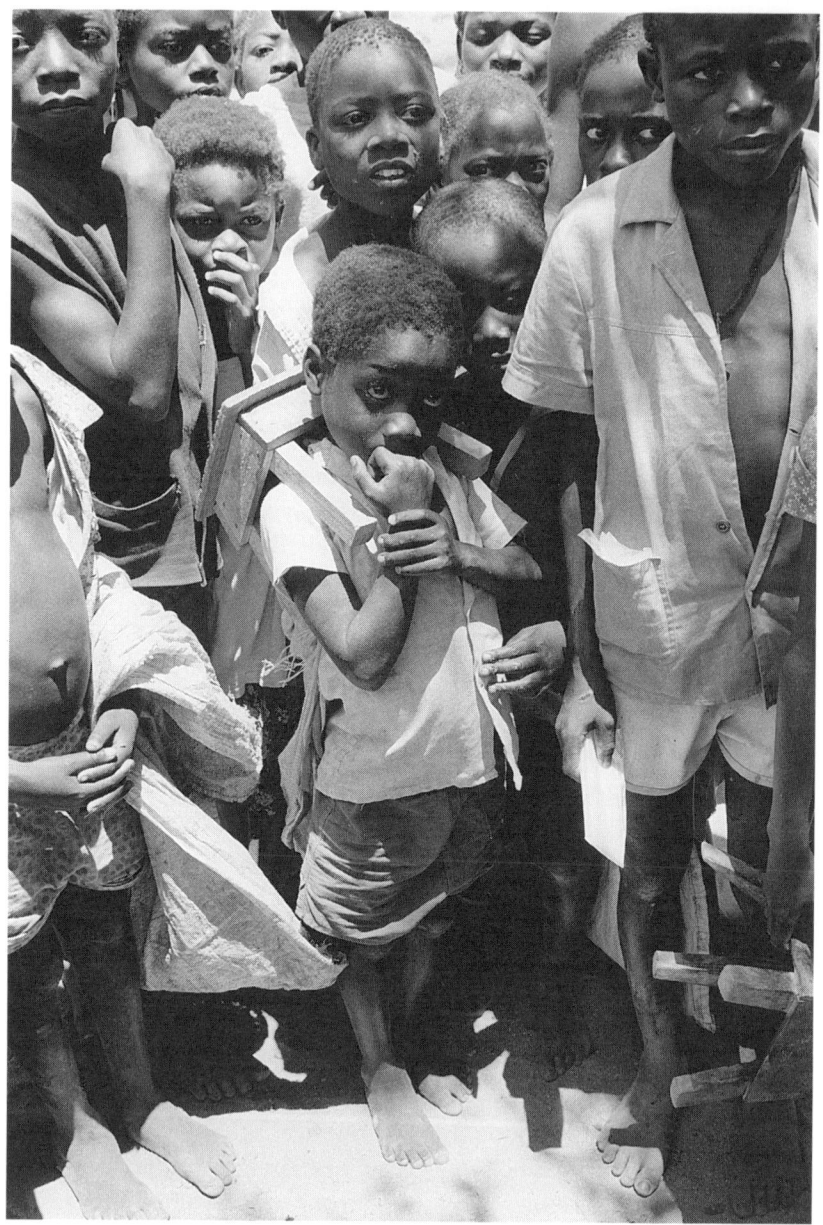

Angolan children bring their own stools to school. Children who don't own a stool have to sit on the floor.

World War II in Japan. Whenever a shop opened, long lines formed outside. Even if people did not know what was for sale they would join the line anyway. That's the sort of thing that happens in wartime.

Angola had been a Portuguese colony for almost five hundred years. I was told by a government official that when the country became independent in 1975, barely fifteen percent of the people could read. In most of the Portuguese colonies, only a small minority enjoyed the privilege of education. It was the same in Mozambique, where only two percent of the people could read and write at the time they gained independence. Still, they managed to achieve their independence, proving that the educational factor was not crucial to political freedom.

Even after independence, the civil war raged on. The young men became soldiers, while those left behind had to keep on fleeing. Consequently, education could not make the progress that was hoped for. Added to this, there was an overwhelming shortage of teachers.

Doctors were a rarity. There were only 750 doctors for ten million people. (In Japan, there are 17,500 doctors for the same number of people, according to the 1992 census.) And of those 750 doctors, 450 were from Cuba, as part of an aid program, which would be ending soon, leaving only 300 doctors behind for the same ten million people. It goes without saying that medicine, too, was in short supply.

To make matter worse, a great many people were suffering from malnutrition. The year I was there, two million people were affected. Not only the children, but the soldiers at the front were also underfed, because provisions could not reach them on account of land mines and guerrilla attacks. Trucks were short of gasoline, too. Money was being used for the war, and there was none left for civilian transport.

A Bouquet of Flowers

The military hospital was packed with soldiers who had lost their legs from land mines. There were others, too, whose sight had been lost in mortar attacks. The blind soldiers were awfully thin. The doctor explained that their skinniness was caused by malnutrition.

I asked some young soldiers of about eighteen or nineteen what sort of work they would like to do when the war ended. They all said that as soon as they were discharged from hospital, they wanted to go back to school and study some more. One land mine victim, limbless from the knees down, with fresh blood oozing onto his bandages, opened his eyes and said, "When the war's over, I want to study and then work in a hospital." How wonderful, I thought, looking into the eyes of the young soldier, who was little more than a boy.

None of the soldiers had had any contact with their family. They had no idea what had happened to their homes or whether their parents were alive. And, of course, the parents knew nothing of their children's whereabouts, either. "Everything is in a terrible state," they said. "One can't even write, as one wouldn't know where to send the letter."

A young soldier, with half of his face in bandages because one of his eyes had been gouged out by a mortar shell, presented me with a bouquet on behalf of the others. It consisted of a sunflower, a hibiscus and a sprig of Madagascar periwinkle. Instead of a ribbon, they were tied with a bandage. I wondered where they could have found the flowers in a desolate wasteland with no sign of any flowers anywhere. I thought that bouquet was the loveliest I had ever received. I can still picture the single beautiful eye of that young soldier as he timidly handed it to me.

The Orthopedic Limb Volunteers

Mozambique's civil war had left many injured by land mines. Yet the number of injured was even greater in Angola.

An incredible fifty thousand Angolans had lost arms and legs in land mine accidents. This represents the largest proportion—in terms of total population—of land mine victims in the world. An ugly example of the horrors of land mines.

At the orthopedic rehabilitation center, I met a young mother from a farm, who had been injured by a land mine. This young mother was waiting her turn for an artificial leg. She said she had been working in the fields with her two children, aged eight and two, when she trod on a mine. It had not been there the day before. Her right leg was blown off and her two children killed. Her husband had been killed in the war. She had no family left. She was a robust woman with large eyes, and when I put my hand on her shoulder to comfort her, I couldn't think what to say.

An adult treads on a land mine and loses a limb; that's bad enough, but adults generally survive. Small children, however, invariably die. If death is not instant, the tetanus that is introduced into the wound will almost certainly do for them in time. The shock of the explosion causes brain damage in many children. Shrapnel robs many others of their eyesight. Still more are made deaf by the noise of the detonations.

At the school for the deaf in Luanda, there were children who were learning not sign language but lip reading. It looked very difficult indeed. Chairs were absent from this school, too. The children sat on empty powdered-milk cans and other makeshift seats.

During the previous nine years 500,000 people had been killed in Angola's civil war. Of these, 330,000 were children. When one hears the words "civil war," one tends to think of only soldiers being killed. This is not the case, however. Out of every thousand children, 375 were dying before the age of five from illness and war-related causes. That is four out of ten. And for every child that dies, a mother cries her heart out.

Angola had the highest children's death rate in the world.

The estimated number of orphans was said to be 150,000. This was far more than the orphanages could cope with.

I was immensely impressed with the Center, a project undertaken by Sweden in Angola, with all its dangers. It was just what was needed most by the Angolans. The Center had about three rooms and was staffed by four young Swedish artificial-limb technicians, who were there as part of the aid program. They were surrounded by malaria and tetanus, and the water was bad. In spite of such terrible hygiene conditions, there they were, working hard for the local people.

A beautiful blond technician was carefully measuring an amputee. Each artificial leg has to be custom made, which involves a lot of work. They are made by shaping wood, and must be exactly the same size as the amputee's remaining good leg. They are not mass-produced. A technician working very hard can only fit between fifteen and twenty amputees with artificial legs in one day. Every artificial leg made enables somebody to walk.

After making inquiries, I discovered, to my amazement, that many countries had sent people to help. None of the various orphanages I visited were set up by the Angolan government—they had all been founded by foreign governments or private organizations.

Japan is considered rich. We send money rather than people. This, I think, is because we are not accustomed to doing the necessary research into what is needed most, as the Swedes had done. If the Japanese government did so, I think they would find lots of people who would be only too happy to do things like making artificial limbs, digging wells, serving as nurses, and hugging and comforting orphans.

Where Is the Safe Toilet?

Luanda was safe because of the soldiers guarding the city. Outside the city, one never could be sure what might happen.

It was arranged that we should go to Benguela, a province 250 miles south of Luanda. The roads were too dangerous because of the land mines and guerrilla raids, so we had to fly there in small airplanes. There were no regular domestic flights; UNICEF had to charter the aircraft. The man in the UNICEF office said he had had the most difficult time in his life chartering those planes. There were no pilots prepared to run the risk of encountering land mines or guerrilla attacks on landing.

From the airport, we went on by car. The car I was in was escorted by a vehicle full of soldiers armed with machine guns in the front and a gunner at the rear. On our way, we passed by a rather large hillock on which a row of soldiers stood with guns. Without that kind of guard, we could not have gone to Benguela.

I was sternly instructed that if I wanted to use the toilet, I would have to tend to my needs right by the car. If I went off into the grass by the side of the road, there might be a land mine there. Indeed, the only safe place was the road that had been driven over by the car in front. I did not drink anything before or during the ride and made up my mind to do my utmost not to want to go. It would certainly not do for the UNICEF goodwill ambassador to lower her slacks at the side of the car. As for public toilets, there were none at all in any of the countries I visited.

The Benguela Railway, Africa's longest, boasted a length of 1,250 miles. It was now in ruins from land mines, except for a nineteen-mile section on which trains could still run. Its terminus was Lobito Port Station, once part of an active port until the guerrillas destroyed it. At the railroad station, inoperative locomotives were lined up in a row. They were unusable because they had been blown up by time bombs and destroyed beyond repair. There were only ten working and running locomotives.

When we were driving along in the car, after leaving Lobito Port, I saw a train stopped right in the middle of the plain. It looked as if it were about to start, and someone was blowing the whistle. It remained motionless in what looked like just an expanse of grass but, apparently, that was the station. There was no platform or anything. It was like a bus stop.

The train was packed tight with children and adults. Crowds of people were clinging on, just as they used to do in Japan right after the war. The people were not just in the passenger cars but in the freight cars, too, all packed in like sardines. In spite of the overcrowding, the first three carriages—all open freight cars—were empty. I couldn't understand why these three cars were not carrying passengers. I was told the gruesome reason. Those first three cars were left empty to protect the rest of the train from any land mines. If the train should run over a mine, only these three front cars would be blown up. Everyone, indeed, was living in close proximity with death.

In June that year, I heard that the government had signed a cease-fire with the guerrillas. I wondered what that would mean.

Arms and Legs Hacked off

Fifty miles outside Benguela, we arrived at a refugee camp that seemed to be in the middle of a desert. There were two thousand refugees there. Each of the 350 mud huts housed anywhere from seven to eight family members. UNICEF was showing the families how to plant crops. Green leaves had begun to appear, but I was told planting was very difficult, owing to the shortage of hoes and plows, coupled with a general lack of water.

As the refugee camp was near the front line, many of the children there had lived through terrible experiences.

The antigovernment guerrillas, who planted land mines and took part in armed raids, belonged to an organization called the Union for the Total Independence of Angola (UNITA), which was backed by South Africa. As mentioned earlier, South Africa supported the guerrillas because it thought that successful black rule in Angola and Mozambique would pose a threat to its own system of apartheid. The local people believed that South Africa's armed forces were so superbly equipped that even the combined forces of all the neighboring countries could not defeat them. That was the kind of backing the UNITA guerrillas had.

What these rebels were doing in Angola was different from the guerrilla activities in the other countries I had visited. The men would first loot the houses of the farmers at harvest time. Next, they would kill the father, if he was there. Then they would rape the mother and, if they liked her, carry her away. Any girls or boys of workable age would be abducted for forced labor. Up to that point, they conducted themselves in much the same way as the guerrillas in Mozambique. What was so much crueler about these people was that if the mother had a baby in her arms, they would tell her to throw it to them, then cut off its arms and legs with a macheté. Small children would be bound with rope to a tree, where the guerrillas would again do their business with their machetés and slice off the young captives' arms. The children were left to die. Any survivors ended up as limbless orphans, dependents for the rest of their lives.

There was a pretty girl about eight years old, with her hair in

ANGOLA, 1989

A girl whose arms were cut off by guerrillas. She said friends had plaited her hair for her.

lots of tiny braids that framed her face. Her arms were gone from the shoulder. The guerrillas had cut them off with a macheté when she was an infant, after murdering both her parents. I hesitated to ask her, but boldly did so: "Do you remember it happening?"

"I don't remember very much. That's when they killed my mother and father," she replied in a hardly audible voice, with lowered eyes.

A boy who showed me his crude artificial left leg had had the leg slashed away with a macheté, too. When asked about it, he shut his mouth tight and refused to talk.

A lad who had not managed to run away fast enough had been tied to a tree. Both his arms had been severed at the shoulder. That child told me about it in detail. Perhaps the guerrillas did these things to scare people and show off their power. Those poor children, who had done nothing, were forced to spend the rest of their lives with disabled bodies! Orphans of slaughtered parents. And children continued to be born into that awful situation.

I prayed with all my heart that peace would come soon to Angola and that the country could be restored to health.

Both the president and the prime minister said, "We are giving priority to the happiness of the children. But we have nothing, so there is nothing we can do for them. So we're working with all our might for freedom. That will bring them happiness."

Having been to many places in Angola and seen many things, I didn't think the two men were lying.

A Dance of Welcome

In spite of such tribulations, the people of Angola were remarkably cheerful, or should I say stalwart.

Among the people I met, whether educated or otherwise, I never heard a single person shout or create a commotion. They were all soft-spoken and gentle and had a sense of humor.

I was once at a camp with about two thousand refugees who had been driven away from their homes because of the warfare going on in their native villages. All the camps had a mixture of men, women and children. At this one, for some reason, the children, the women and the men welcomed me separately.

I first shook hands with the children. Then I shook hands with the women. The women announced that they were going to perform a welcome dance, and immediately broke into an impassioned dance. Twittering like birds in very high voices, then singing a song in powerful tones, they all danced with tremendous energy. They had no musical instruments. They kept time by clapping with their hands and stamping with their feet so hard that the ground shook.

With the scorching sun beating down on the desert, it was over 105 degrees and terribly hot. I was afraid the women would all get sunstroke. Elderly women were dancing too.

In the middle of this neverending welcome, I started walking off to see the camp dwellings with the TV crew. As I did so, the man in charge of taking us around came after me.

"Miss Kuroyanagi, you shook hands with the children and the women, but you haven't shaken hands with the men. They are very upset. Do please come and greet them."

"Oh dear," I said, "I didn't, did I. Well, you see, the dancing started so soon...."

I went back and said to the men, "Do please forgive me. I didn't mean to leave you out. It was because the dancing started. It was very rude of me."

Then I shook hands with each of them. Most were elderly, and they were all squatting on the ground with their heads down, moving their fingers about in the sand as if they were writing something. That's when I was made very aware of the difference between the men and the women. It is often said that women are the stronger sex, and in this country, too, they really seemed to me to be so. The women danced and sang for three hours in that scorching heat. When I left and waved good-bye to them, they were still dancing. And I don't think they had had very much to eat. Their energy was amazing.

I suppose women are more realistic and matter-of-fact about life. Many had lost their homes, their husbands and their children. But they were able to dance for the sheer joy of being alive. "Today, let's dance!" "Today, let's join forces and get the work done!" "Let's enjoy life whenever we can!" That was the impression they gave.

Compared with the women, it seemed that the men were clinging to their ideals and unable to come to terms with reality. The old men had lost their homes just when they would have had grandchildren, profited by their sons' independence, and reached the age where they could take it easy. But their sons had died in the war. It had all gone wrong, and they wondered what would become of them now. The shock was so great they couldn't rise above things. Although their lives were safe in the refugee camp, they were mired in despondency.

Back in the capital, we visited the port in the center of Luanda just as the sun, like a large ball of fire, was about to sink into the sea. From this port, I was told, nine million Angolan slaves were transported to the American continent.

So this was the country from which millions of able-bodied young men in their prime, with a future before them, were shipped. The same thing happened in other African countries, too. What an achievement to become independent after all they must have gone through!

What We Want Most Is Freedom!

The reason I continue as a UNICEF goodwill ambassador is because I want as many people as possible to know about the children in the world who are in need of aid. Naturally, I, too, want to learn about those children.

As I always do at the end of my visit, I went to a sort of public park and faced the TV camera to give my impressions of the country. The children who were gathered around me were so excited they began lustily singing a song together that went "Cha, Cha, Angola!" I had to raise my voice to be heard. I began, "This is the end of my visit to Angola." But the children kept on singing, so I only managed to get a few words in edgeways.

On my visits to Africa up until then, there had been many crowds of children who did not even have the strength to cry. It was nice to find children who were hale and hearty. They were all so attractive, too, with sweet, innocent faces, undaunted by the dreadful conditions around them. When I asked children in the various parts of

Angola that I visited what they needed most, nobody mentioned things like food. They all answered "Freedom." And it was definitely not just a show of courage; nor was it something they had been told to say.

To see such young children drawing themselves up straight and saying "Freedom" made one truly want to give them something to hope for.

By coincidence, that night I attended a dinner to which all the ambassadors had been invited. We ate in semidarkness, owing to a power cut. In the middle of the dinner, an announcement came through that the Berlin Wall had fallen. Everyone stood up and cheered, and the ambassadors agreed that Gorbachev should receive the Nobel Prize. Clapping went on for a long time, and it was a heartwarming evening. "Might the fall of the Berlin Wall and consequent East-West rapprochement mean that, in its turn, South Africa will stop supporting the guerrillas?" I wondered.

The people of Angola had been sacrificing a great deal for freedom and peace, something it is hard for the rest of us to comprehend, so accustomed are we to peace. But I understood well what the president meant when he said they had nothing else to work for. I thought so, too, as I took my leave of Angola.

CHAPTER SEVEN

BANGLADESH, 1990

IN 1990, I VISITED BANGLADESH, said to be the poorest country, not only in Asia, but in the whole world. It is on the northeastern border with India, on the Bay of Bengal. Its size is 55,598 square miles.

According to the 1990 census, 113 million people live there. The population is about the same as that of Japan except that, amazingly, almost half of Bangladesh's population (about 53.5 million) is made up of children under the age of sixteen. Child mortality is very high. About nine hundred thousand children under the age of five die each year. That amounts to about twenty-four hundred deaths a day, or as many as a hundred children an hour. There is great rejoicing if a child reaches the age of five. At the risk of sounding repetitive, but for the sake of comparative illustration, in Japan, a country whose population is roughly the same size, nine thousand children under the age of five die each year, as opposed to Bangladesh's nine hundred thousand.

Each Flood Puts a Third of the Country Underwater

Known for its fertile soil and consistently good harvests, Bangladesh used to be called Golden Bengal. *Bangladesh* simply means the "place where the Bengalis live." The language is also called Bengali. The staple food is rice, which can be harvested three times a year. Bengali farmers, however, lead a very hard life. As very few actually own their land, almost all their harvest is used to pay the rent. Not even enough rice is left for the family. Their only option is to move to the towns to try to find work that will bring in some money. It must be said, though, that—unlike India—there is no significant gap between the rich and the poor.

Hardship is not new to the Bengalis. The people have always been poor. In every era, the blessings of prosperity have been snatched away from them, precisely because it was fit to be called Golden Bengal. It happened under the British Raj, and it happened after independence from Britain and separation from India, when the territory became part of Pakistan. Then in 1971, following a war for independence in which three million people were killed, they finally won their freedom, through bloodshed. Yet the country had been ruined by the war, and over ten million people fled to India as refugees.

On a memorial to the war dead are these words: "The blood of heroes and warriors and the tears of mothers, both shed for this land in vain. The price we paid was great enough to have bought Paradise."

The words overflow with the grief of the people.

A series of floods and natural disasters have hindered Bangladesh's efforts toward economic recovery since independence. Roughly ninety percent of the country is made up of land that lies thirty feet above sea level. Nothing can stop an overflowing river in these circumstances.

Satellite photographs show that Bangladesh's waterways form a complex web of rivers, whose waters are supplied by melted snow from the Himalayas as well as from local rainfall. The volume of water flowing into this network of rivers is accordingly extremely high. Indeed, just one flood will inundate at least one-third of the country. Is there any other country where one-third of it disappears underwater each time there is a flood? Bangladesh is tragically well known for its floods.

Our first destination was Comilla, which we set off for by car on a fifty-five mile trip from Dhaka, the capital.

After driving for twenty minutes, we came to the Meghna River, which has to be crossed by ferry. Unlike most rivers elsewhere, the Meghna had no sloping margin or embankment, and its waters were almost level with its rim. Indeed, the river even looked higher than the land beside it, when viewed from ground level. "It's no wonder that the houses by the river get washed away when there's a flood," I thought, "and the water flows right into the middle of the towns." The prohibitively high cost of building embankments along the length of the river would have rendered any such project unfeasible.

Only two years before our trip, a particularly monstrous flood had put two-thirds of Bangladesh underwater and inflicted damage on the person or property of forty million inhabitants. Ninety percent of Dhaka was flooded. The year after we were there, I read in the paper that the country had suffered another deluge and a cyclone which caused almost one hundred forty thousand fatalities. There would be chaos in Japan if that number of people were killed all at once! According to a UNICEF report on that flood, the winds were so strong that mothers tried unsuccessfully to prevent their children from being blown away by tying them to the trees. Sadly, the formidable power of the storm uprooted the trees themselves and swept the poor children away.

Violent storms do not stop at taking human lives, and Bangladesh's crops were also ruined. Such natural disasters are a major cause of famine, illness and poverty there. Ironically, the same floods give the country its fertile soil, so ideal for agriculture. The farmers of the delta must make a living growing things in the midst of this paradox.

Shaking Hands

We drove some thirty minutes from Comilla to visit an area of farming villages. At the entrance to a village called Chandsree, there was a bridge over a stream that consisted of a single bamboo pole. In the old days in Japan, there were quite a few bridges of this sort. I used to take pride in crossing them as a child, so was quite undaunted. I took off my shoes and ran across. A young newspaper correspondent who was with me chickened out and shouted that he couldn't cross. I felt a bit mean but called back, teasingly, "You won't get your stories if you don't come over!" The bridge was not all that high. It was only about ten feet above the water.

The village children were delighted that I had crossed so easily. They were all thin and wore crude outfits. But their smiles were beautiful. I never expected to find them all so wonderfully bright and cheerful.

The children were all busy working. Girls were carrying bundles of firewood on their heads. Boys balanced sacks of harvested rice at each end of a pole, which they bore atop their shoulders. These sacks looked heavier than they actually were. To help with the insufficient housekeeping money, children worked from the time they were small, sometimes not even going to school.

I saw a boy working hard collecting cow dung for use as fuel. "Hello!" I said to him. "You've collected quite a lot, haven't you?"

I held out my hand to shake his, but he noticed he had some dung on it, and he seemed to hesitate, wondering what to do. He then made up his mind and shook my hand. I showed him the muck that had got on my hand and said in Japanese, "What shall I do about this?" He must have understood, because he laughed. His smile was sweet, unclouded.

Other children who had been watching from a distance came over and surrounded me. They were all very friendly and inquisitive.

When I said, "Come on, let's shake hands," to the other kids, holding out my hand with the cow dung on it, they all shook their heads and ran away. Even the children collecting cow dung with their hands obviously knew it wasn't clean.

The first Bengali word the children taught me was *dhonnobad* ("thank you"). Most of them could neither read nor write; neither could their parents. Literacy in Bangladesh was forty-two percent for men and twenty-two percent for women. Altogether, thirty percent of the population was literate.

The Grameen Bank

Poverty was not the only serious challenge facing Bangladesh. Sexual discrimination had put Bengali women in frustratingly difficult circumstances. For instance, a family would only send its sons to school, because they would be the future breadwinners. Similarly, the boys always got plenty to eat. It was taboo for women to have an education or hold a gathering in a public place. These old customs are still observed today.

The dowry system is one tragic example of ill treatment and discrimination against women in Bangladesh. As in India, a Bangladeshi bride must present her husband's family with a dowry of goods or property or a cash equivalent. Although it is supposed to be against the law, a wife who comes from a family too poor to provide an adequate dowry will often suffer cruelty at the hands of her husband and mother-in-law. In the end, she may be thrown out or, in the worst possible scenario, beaten to death. There have even been cases where a husband has set his wife's sari on fire and left her to die in the flames. For whatever reasons, these vile crimes regularly go unpunished. That is why, especially in peasant families, the birth of a girl is a great disappointment.

Bangladeshi women must live in truly pathetic conditions. A wife is not free to go out. Even the shopping is done by the husband. Few husbands earn enough to live comfortably, and many women would be willing to work in order to supplement the family income. Unfortunately there are few places where they can find jobs. It was like that in my own country in years gone by.

But nowadays the women have a friend and ally. There is a bank that makes loans to women, to help them become independent. It is called the Grameen Bank (*grameen* means "rural"). It charges normal interest, but no collateral is required, and it lends money on trust. Before the arrival of the Grameen Bank, of course, no other banks would lend money to women without funds or collateral.

The bank was started by the economist Dr. Muhammad Yunus, of Bangladesh, with thirty dollars of his own money. In only fourteen years, it became the Grameen Bank, doing 220 million dollars worth of business. Ninety-four percent of the borrowers are poor women.

A bank just for the poor! Isn't that marvelous?

Dr. Yunus was a charming man. He patiently described to me how he started the bank with almost nothing. What impressed me particularly was the fact that he had confidence in women. Wanting to give some independence to women, who were not allowed even to go out, he started by dividing thirty dollars among forty-two farm women, and suggested they invest the money in chickens. When the chickens began to lay eggs, the women were to sell the eggs. He then taught them how to save the money little by little.

Dr. Yunus trusted the women because his experience in lending money to men was that many did not honor their promises. When the day came to pay back the money, it might all have evaporated, spent on drink. Whereas women, particularly poor women, were meticulous about paying interest on the appointed day. Moreover, Dr. Yunus got the women to form themselves into groups, so that in case anyone wasn't able to repay her loan on time, someone in her group could lend her the money. He knew it would be to their advantage for them to help one another.

The women started by selling eggs. As the quantity of chickens increased, they expanded to selling chickens, too. Though the women stayed at home, they began making money. Eventually they invested in sheep, and then cattle. Profits that may seem small from a Western point of view are a lot in Bangladesh. The Grameen Bank system has been a useful example to many countries in the world.

Although he lent money to the poor only, Dr. Yunus, in the fourteen-year span from 1976 to 1990, parlayed a capital of thirty dollars into a 220-million-dollar business, which goes to show the significance of small profits. It also shows that once they have some money of their own, there is no telling how far women can advance.

In order to make money calculations, however, women first need to learn arithmetic. They must learn to read, too. Soon the women will realize that education is essential for their children, and they will be able to pay for it with the money they have earned themselves. That is when they will begin to turn their eyes toward society, and everything will begin to improve.

In one village we visited, one of these Grameen Bank women's groups happened to be having a meeting. They were all women who had never managed any cash in their lives before. I joined the group and asked the women for their opinions. They were positive.

"My husband lets me come to these meetings now."

"My husband, who went to Dhaka to work and didn't return, has come back now."

"My husband looks after the children now."

A woman who borrowed money six times from the Grameen Bank and made a success out of her livestock business said, happily, "My daughter-in-law says she wants me to live with them." She was very wrinkled and looked old, but when I asked her age, she said she was forty-five. The women at the meeting were all brimming with confidence and had lively expressions.

I felt that great things were ahead for Bangladesh, now that the women were starting to want to change things.

The bank's founder was also optimistic: "We are trying to change people's lives through the Grameen Bank. We are extending a helping hand to people without money or property to mortgage. Now, almost ninety-eight percent of the 850,000 people with loans are repaying them on time. We haven't had to take anybody to court or call in the police to make people repay their loans. This proves that even poor people can do things if they make up their minds to. The same principles can be applied anywhere in the world."

How fortunate they were to have an economist who was such a man of action! How encouraging! The only banks I had known up to then were ones that catered to the rich. Step-by-step progress made by trusting the poor and seeing that people can repay their loans promptly—whether on a personal or national basis—is a great development.

Watch Your Step!

We visited a slum in the center of Dhaka, in an area called Komolaphr. There were about a thousand people living in this slum. Most of them had fled there from farming villages when their homes were washed away in a flood.

I had a real shock when I saw the slum. People were living right in the midst of mountains of garbage, which emitted smoke from burning methane gas. The smell was so awful I don't know how to describe it. Even the people who lived there had to hold their noses as they passed close by. There were 1,125 of these slums in Dhaka. Forty percent of the capital city's population of 4,770,000 live in them. I found it hard to believe and tried to imagine forty percent of the people of Tokyo living in the middle of a mountain of refuse.

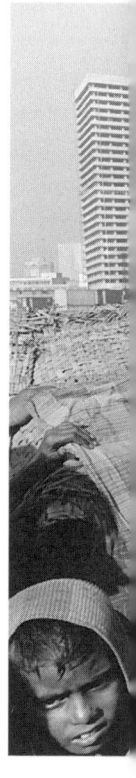

Children, with bags, were poking through the garbage with sticks, trying to find anything they could either use or eat. There wasn't a single item of the kind of "big trash" one finds so much of in Japan. There wasn't even a single plastic bag. If one had been thrown away, it would instantly have been picked up by a child and sold to a collector of waste materials. Here and there were puddles of water full of creepy-crawlies, and there were lots of flies, too. Even in such an environment, though, the children were very attractive and full of curiosity.

They would come up to me and touch me or grasp my hands and not let go. Little five-year-old Wasim, whom I picked up and held in my arms, put his arms around my neck and tightly held on to my blouse. He was suffering from malnutrition, and his tummy was swollen. His mother said he had had blood in his stool for a long time. She was very worried. Malnutrition and bloody stools: that sounded really bad. His mother apparently didn't have the money to take him to a doctor and didn't know what to do.

In slums like this, two hundred out of one thousand infants die before they are a year old. It is no wonder. There were no wells nearby, and a pot of clean water cost forty cents.

Wasim was the second youngest of five children. They lived in a crude hut made of wood scraps and sheets of galvanized iron. There was hardly room for the family to sleep. The floor was of bare earth. The household goods consisted of a small straw mat, a cooking pot and a pot for water. Nothing else. All the dwellings were the same.

Daily living expenses amounted to seven or eight taka (about thirty cents). There were some days when the family did not have a

BANGLADESH, 1990

Myself holding Wasim. His mother is on my right with her other children. Behind us is their house.

meal at all. In spite of their lifestyle, however, the mother was very proud of the fact that two of her children went to school. When I heard that even in a slum like this, the families were obliged to pay rent for their homes, I was truly astounded. The rent per month in their area ranged from 350 to 400 taka (fourteen to sixteen dollars).

In all this, the saving grace was the cheerfulness of the children. They were very good at imitating what I said. Whenever I called out to Mr. Tanuma, our photographer, they would immediately imitate me and all shout together, in their sweet little voices, "Ta-nu-ma-saaan!" I stepped in some feces of some sort that was in among the garbage. When the children pointed to it, I said, "Better watch your step!" in Japanese. They repeated this tricky phrase too, all together. Here, in the worst possible conditions, I wondered how the children managed to produce such dazzling smiles. Their whole attitude to life, in fact, was tough and resolutely forward-looking.

The inhabitants of this slum were under orders from the police to evacuate. It was soon to be demolished. This meant the children would be moving to an even worse environment. I said a silent prayer for them: "Please be strong and don't lose your cheerfulness."

The *Pathakali* Schools

A surprising thing happened while I was in Bangladesh, following an interview with the president, Mohammed Ershad. My meeting with him was my last commitment in Bangladesh. I went straight from there to the airport.

During the interview, the president had spoken earnestly about the problems of his country and the children's future.

President Ershad had held the reins of power for just over eight years and eight months. However, he had been confronted by the opposition and the people with a harsh demand for his resignation, and, by coincidence, at the very moment I left Bangladesh he was arrested and remanded in custody. This sudden turn of events meant we couldn't use the specially televised scene of our meeting, which in its own way showed how political unrest can affect the welfare of children.

I had heard that the city of Dhaka was crowded, but the multitudes I saw were even greater than I had imagined. The city overflowed with cars and rickshaws and people in a melee of congestion. Rickshaws (tricycles pedaled by foot, with a rear seat for passengers) were used as taxis. The quickest way someone from a farming village who was looking for work could earn money was as a driver of one of these. In Dhaka alone, there were 96,000 registered rickshaws. As they were said to be used on a double-shift system, a simple calculation shows that there must be 192,000 drivers. I remember meeting quite a few children in various places who said their fathers were rickshaw drivers.

Most of the drivers rent their rickshaws. They have to give fifteen taka (about sixty cents) out of a day's earnings to the owner, leaving a take-home salary of only fifty taka (about two dollars) or so each day. I had a ride in one. When I heard that as many as four fat middle-aged women get in sometimes, with large bundles, I thought what hard pedaling that must be for the poor driver.

To help with the household finances, many children do some sort of work. In Dhaka, there are *pathakali* schools to enable working children to study. *Pathakali* means "wayside flower buds," and likens children in disadvantaged environments to flowers that have not yet bloomed. The idea is that these schools help them bloom. The schools were founded and so named by the former president, Mohammed Ershad, who was also a poet. "How nice to have a poet-president," I thought, and regretted whatever it was that brought about his arrest.

The *pathakali* school I visited had six classes, with thirty-five students in each. The school mainly taught how to read and write Bengali, the national language. Tuition was free, and breakfast was provided, as well as medical facilities. There were sixty-five such schools throughout the country, with a total of 13,500 pupils. Since enrollment was limited, there were many children on a waiting list.

Classes were for two hours each day. The children went to work afterward. The pupils were divided into two shifts: those who started work at 10:00 could attend the 7:00 to 9:00 class, while those who started work later could attend the 9:30 to 11:30 class.

When I visited a class, I noticed how earnest all the children were. Not a single child was wasting time chatting.

I also went to see one of the places where *pathakali* pupils worked. If it hadn't been for the lights we set up for the TV cameras, the children would have been working in semidarkness.

In a tiny, hot room that could not have been much more than twelve-by-eight feet, girls of about seven or eight were making cardboard spools for cotton thread, shaped like ice-cream cones. Bangladesh's textile industry earns foreign currency. All the children looked small for their age. They never stopped working. Working without a break for eight hours a day, they manage to make ten taka (about forty cents).

Boys were working in a small factory with a machine that looked like a lathe, tooling some large flat metal to make it shine. They seemed accustomed to the work. One of them said he had been doing it for two years. When I asked his age, he said "Nine." So this child had been working since he was six and a half. All day, standing up. His daily wage, too, was the equivalent of forty cents.

The local man who showed us around said, "This work is not too difficult for children, and it isn't dangerous either. It's easy work."

"It is only a month now until the New Year," I thought, "when Japanese children would be receiving their *otoshidama*, or traditional gift of money." Small children would get at least a one-thousand-yen bank note. Some even get several ten-thousand-yen bills. And here were these children steadily working eight hours a day, without so much as a sideways glance, and only making forty yen, which they cannot even spend on themselves. The whole family depends on all the children's wages. I did not see any of them, but I heard about children whose parents had cut off their arms and legs on purpose, so people would feel sorry for the disabled child, and they could earn a lot of money begging. I heard that this went on not only in Bangladesh, but in India, too.

Vast sums of money are spent on wars in which people kill one another.

According to UNICEF, the cost for work done in the final ten years of the twentieth century to prevent most child-related deaths and malnutrition had been estimated at roughly 2.5 billion dollars per year. This is quite a sum. Yet, this sum is only *two percent of the total expenditure of all the armed forces of the world*. It is also equivalent to the price of five Stealth bombers.

When one thinks of that huge sum of money spent by the military, the forty cents earned by children working all day seems all the more tragic, especially when one recalls that it is the children who will be the mainstays of the next era.

BANGLADESH, 1990

The World's Finest Diarrhea Hospital

Babies were being inoculated at the Kaptan Bazaar Primary School in Comilla. It was part of a grand scheme to promote awareness of inoculation in Bangladesh.

We were welcomed by a group of girls holding banners that illustrated, through pictures, how inoculation could save children from death due to tuberculosis, tetanus, diptheria, whooping cough, polio and measles.

Most children in Bangladesh were born with malnutrition. This is because their mothers had malnutrition themselves and gave birth at a young age. If the babies had been inoculated, three hundred thousand of the nine hundred thousand that normally died each year before reaching the age of five could have been saved. In spite of the campaign, there were still many children who were dying throughout Bangladesh because they had not been able to be inoculated.

Another major cause of infant mortality was diarrhea, due to unhygienic drinking water. One-third of all children's deaths under the age of five was from diarrhea-related diseases.

Transmission of disease was particularly dangerous in times of flood. In addition to the wells becoming unusable, fuel was unobtainable for cooking, and people would drink unboiled water that had been contaminated with dust and dirt. The government warned people not to drink water from flooded rivers, with posters saying, "Only drink water that has been boiled." They also tried to provide clean water, but this did not have much effect. Many lives continue to be lost because the people continue to drink water in which animal carcasses have been floating alongside human excrement.

We visited the hospital attached to the International Center for Diarrheal Disease Research. This fine hospital is said to carry out the most advanced research into diarrhea in the world. Quite simply, there is nowhere else like it. Two hundred diarrhea sufferers visit the hospital every day. In March and April, the hottest months, the number of patients swells to almost six hundred a day. There were only two hundred beds, causing patients to overflow into the corridors. Most of the patients were small children.

BANGLADESH, 1990

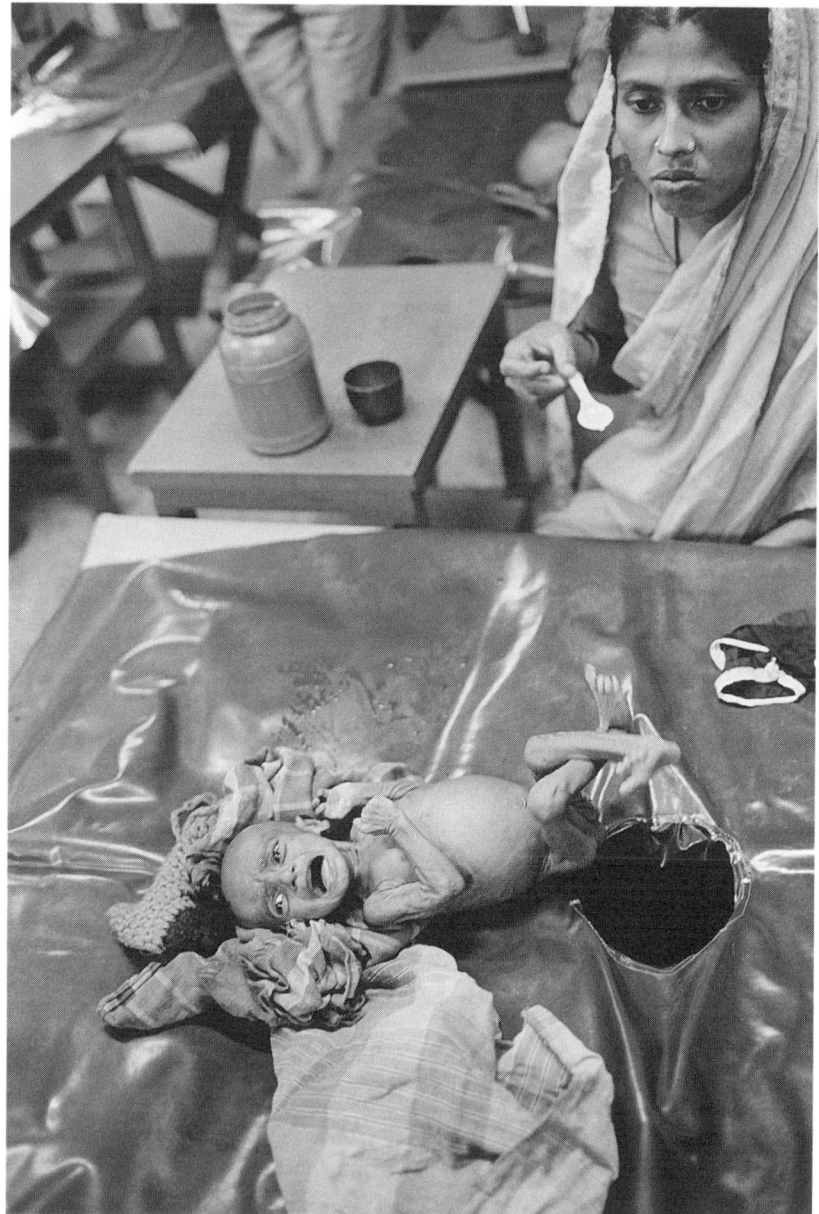

A baby struggling for survival. His wrinkled skin is due to dehydration, a common symptom of acute diarrhea.

BANGLADESH, 1990

In the waiting room for mothers of children with relatively mild cases of diarrhea, a nurse was using graphic panels to teach young mothers about the effectiveness of inoculations and hygiene.

Oral rehydration therapy is a useful treatment in diarrhea. It is very simple: the patient is merely given water to drink in which salt and sugar and other nutrients have been dissolved. This treatment can stop the dehydration caused by diarrhea. UNICEF is propagating this method worldwide, a relatively inexpensive way of preventing deaths from this cause. A packet of oral rehydration salts only costs about a dime.

I entered a ward where children were lying on blue latex sheets, in obvious agony. There was a hole in the middle of each bed to let the loose fecal matter through into a receptacle beneath. Beside each bed stood a worried-looking mother, watching over her child.

Most of the children—including a baby barely four weeks old—were suffering from malnutrition. He was just skin and bones. His skin was as wrinkled as an old man's. The boy was desperately trying to live, crying for all he was worth. He was the tiniest child I had seen at any of the hospitals in the countries I had been to. Any baby as small and sick as that would normally have died. His life had been saved by being in the world's leading diarrhea hospital. He was so small he could have fitted inside my two hands.

One six-year-old girl had been suffering from diarrhea for two months. The diarrhea was being complicated by other diseases as well. She was seized with a convulsion right there before my eyes. But they said she had improved enormously just with tender loving care.

The children who were the most seriously ill were so wasted they did not have the strength to cry. Their eyes, as they stared at me, seemed to be pleading, "I just want to live some more." "I'm so sorry," I murmured under my breath, as I gazed back at those ancient-looking eyes; "I wish I could do something for you. Don't give up!"

A seven-month-old baby had been suffering from constant diarrhea for sixteen days, with a high temperature. He was coughing, too. With swollen feet and a belly distended from malnutrition, he was suffering from a combination of other diseases as well. His condition was very bad. The young mother was crying because she said her baby would not recover. She then laid her cheek on my foot, saying, "Please pray for my baby."

I said to her, "Don't cry. The doctor said the baby would be all right. You must be strong, mother."

Some of the mothers whose babies were in the hospital were very young, only thirteen or fourteen. In most other countries, girls of this age would still be in middle school. I thought, how cruel for such young mothers to be so burdened with worry about their babies.

It was a sight one could hardly bear to look at. But that was the way things were.

Every year in Bangladesh three hundred thousand children were dying from diarrhea-related diseases. Those who could be treated at a hospital were truly fortunate. A great many died with no possibility of any treatment at all.

Bangladesh was certainly confronted with severe conditions. Yet the people faced disaster cheerfully. They put up with today because they believed in tomorrow. And the most wonderful thing was the children. There was not a child who had become lethargic and spiritless. They bubbled over with a will to live. Even the children living amid the mountains of garbage who parroted everything I said. I am so glad I have been to Bangladesh. Once again, I should like to thank the children who welcomed me so warmly and taught me how to live with sincerity and without complaint.

Dhonnobad, thank you. *Dhonnobad*!

CHAPTER EIGHT

IRAQ, 1991

IN THE EARLY HOURS OF JANUARY 17, 1991, the United States and allied forces launched a large-scale air attack on Iraq. It was the beginning of the Persian Gulf War. As I watched the coverage on television, I thought, "There are children down there where they are bombing. I wonder what's happening to them." I also wondered how many houses had become piles of rubble.

The Gulf War ended after about six weeks. Every night the world watched on television as allied missiles and Iraqi Scud countermissiles collided and exploded in the night sky. Three million dollars went up in smoke, each time an Iraqi air defense missile hit its target. (Each missile costs about 1.5 million dollars.) Each time! And what on earth must the total number of missiles used have been? The war also introduced a new term: pinpoint bombing.

Desperate to know what had happened to the children, I left for Iraq toward the end of July 1991, five months after the war had ended.

The First Thing to Disappear Was Powdered Milk

Iraq is located in the southwest corner of Asia. Only a small part of its coastline faces the Persian Gulf. The population in 1991 was 18,317,000. As part of the United Nations-backed economic sanctions imposed against the country, all air travel between Iraq and other countries had been suspended. Simply arriving in Baghdad, the capital, was quite a task.

Standing on a Baghdad street, I found the apparent lack of visible damage to private house surprising. I had expected mountains of rubble and was stunned not to find any. "What about all that bombing I saw on TV?" I wondered.

Making a deliberate effort to look up as I walked, I saw the occasional building that was missing its roof. Walking normally, these things were not noticeable. It did not look a bit like Tokyo in the aftermath of the wartime bombings. I was told that pinpoint bombing only destroyed designated targets. "What exactly were they targeting?" we wondered as we traveled around, having a look at Iraq.

I, who had not minded the 145-degree heat in Africa, was very conscious of the heat here—a humid 122 degrees—and the burning wind blowing in one's face that made it feel even hotter. You can try experiencing it, too: just take a hair dryer, put it on its hottest setting and hold it about two or three feet from your face. Switch it on, and imagine how it would feel blowing on your face all day. That will give you an idea of how hot it was. Do you think you could manage to live in that heat, with no electricity, no running water, no refrigerator or any of the other modern conveniences? Many did, and it was hard for them.

Although memories of the war itself may have faded in the five months since it ended, the conditions that it left behind have been unbearably tough, particularly for the children and their mothers. Shortages of food and powdered milk gave rise to predictions that 170,000 children under the age of five would probably die within six months of malnutrition, diarrhea and other infectious diseases. My trip became a time of wondering how to save as many lives as we could.

We visited a market in Baghdad.

When the Gulf War broke out, Iraq was dependent on imports for seventy percent of its food. Sanctions had been imposed for almost a year and stocks had reached rock bottom. Most of the daily commodities sold in the market came from neighboring Jordan, with a few things from Iran and Turkey.

As sanctions had prohibited all oil exports, there was a rampant black market, which was beyond the control of the government. Moreover, inflation was extreme. The cost of a kilo (2.2 pounds) of meat was equivalent to ten percent of an average man's salary. Many people were out of work. They were selling their belongings in order to buy food, just like the "bamboo-shoot existence" in Japan following the end of the Pacific War, when people shed their treasured possessions in order to eat, as one would pare off the layers of a bamboo shoot before cooking it.

The streets of Baghdad were lined with stores closed for lack of both supplies and customers. There was no sign of anyone on the road that specialized in shops selling traditional copperware, once loud with the sound of hammering.

People only bought the bare essentials for daily survival. Foodstuffs that should have been available on ration, like powdered milk, flour, sugar and cooking oil, were generally unobtainable. Powdered milk had been the first to disappear, they said. It could only be bought on the black market for ten times its prewar price, but few mothers could afford that. Yet, suffering from malnutrition themselves, mothers had no milk of their own with which to nurse their babies. Only twenty-five percent of nursing mothers were said to be able to produce any milk. That is, one in four. It was said there were mothers whose milk stopped, owing to fright from the bombing. Consequently, a third of all Iraqi babies were undernourished.

Fruit was about the only thing available in abundance. The market was full of figs, grapes, apples, pears and oranges. The only imported fruit was bananas. But fruit is expensive.

The Consequences of No Electricity

As we walked along the main street in Baghdad, I noticed a strange smell. It was a sewer overflowing onto the street, and it contained fecal matter.

Accurate pinpoint bombing had destroyed all the power plants. The sewer pumps had stopped with the total loss of electricity. The sewer pipes became blocked with filth and burst. Damage like this

IRAQ, 1991

When the power plants were put out of action by the bombs, the sewers broke down and effluent started flowing into people's houses.

had occurred in 472 places in Baghdad alone, and it was impossible to repair. This is why the streets were flooded. The dirty water had flowed into the houses, too.

"See how the sewage has come into my house!" a mother tearfully complained to us.

The ground floor of her house was awash in filth. It was just like a flood. No one could live there. She said they were living upstairs. Upstairs turned out to be the roof. They were, in fact, living out of doors. There was no furniture of any sort, and no roof over their heads. There was nothing but a mattress. In the daytime, the mercury would rise to over 105 degrees. There was nothing on the roof to provide any shade.

The mother showed me her tiny infant's body. Because of the heat, its skin was covered with eczema which looked like prickly heat blisters.

The water supply had also been affected by the loss of power. Without electricity the pumps stopped pumping drinking water to people's homes.

Before the war everyone in the city had electricity and running water. Iraq, after all, had been a relatively prosperous oil-producing country. The abundant waters of the Tigris, the river that flows through Baghdad used to be purified and piped to every household. But because all the power plants had been bombed, it was now impossible to purify the water and convey it to the houses. There was no water coming out of the taps. People had no choice but to go down and fetch the water themselves from the Tigris, and drink it as it was. The problem was compounded by the fact that the sewers emptied into the Tigris. Without electricity, there was no treatment of the sewage.

Almost all Iraq was affected. There was no fuel for boiling the water; neither were there any chemicals for purification. Ongoing economic sanctions prohibited their export to Iraq. Conditions were unhygienic in the extreme. And the children are always the first to suffer. An increasing number had contracted infectious diseases, such as typhoid fever and diarrhea.

IRAQ, 1991

A Baby's Eyes

I visited the Qadissiya Central Hospital in Baghdad. It was only 9:40 in the morning, but the temperature was already over 105 degrees. It would get hotter and rise to 122 degrees. In all that heat, mothers with children were waiting their turn to see a doctor.

The hospital had nothing: no milk, no medicines, no anesthetics for operations. Supplies had reached rock bottom. With no electricity, vaccines for inoculation could no longer be refrigerated and lost their efficacy. Said one of the doctors, "There is nothing more frustrating for a doctor than to make a diagnosis and not be able to treat the disease. One may want to operate, but one cannot, because there is no electricity. Can you understand how hard it is for me simply to say nothing and just watch a child die?"

There was a baby girl only three months old whose mouth and cheeks were so wrinkled from malnutrition that she had a face like an old woman. Her legs were as skinny as a pair of chopsticks. Her mother was so nutritionally deficient that she could produce no milk. All she could give her baby was sugar water. One reason she looked so old was because her eyes were not soft and wet. They were different from the babies I had seen in Japan, whose eyes were wet and shiny like fresh black soybeans. This poor baby had dry eyes, the eyes of an old person coming to the end of life. There was another reason I thought her eyes looked so old. I could feel them looking at me, directly and severely. I was being scrutinized. Sometimes this pair of eyes would accuse me, as if they were saying, "Why has this happened to me?"

Doomed to die so soon, it seemed to me, she wanted to see as much as she could of life in every instant that was left to her. Maybe that's why her eyes looked so mature. The longer I held her gaze, the more I came to that conclusion. How pitiful it was. To have come all the way into this world only to depart so quickly. Who knows, a child like her might have had the genius to save all the children in the world but for the fact that she was born into this country and these circumstances, destined to die looking like a crumpled old rag.

There was never anything one could do to comfort them. All one could do was squeeze their tiny hands and ask in one's heart for

IRAQ, 1991

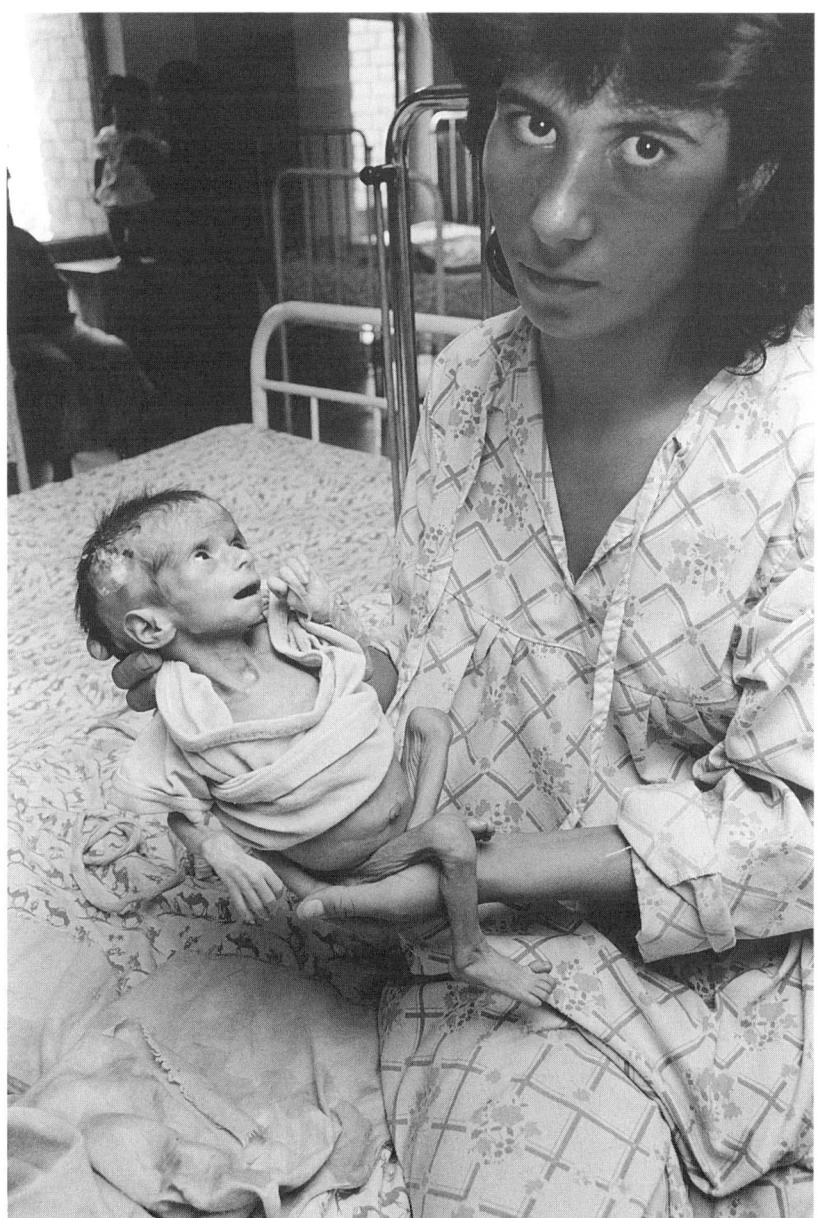

A baby gazes hard at her mother. She is suffering from malnutrition and her eyes have become like those of an old person.

their forgiveness: forgiveness for being able to do nothing to alleviate their plight.

Children can be saved from malnutrition and diseases such as diarrhea, meningitis, typhoid and polio, if only powdered milk, medicines and vaccines for inoculation are made available. Without them, doctors told me they were helpless, and hospital beds remained empty. There was no point in admitting patients when nothing could be done for them. In most cases, they were just turned away.

I met Prime Minister Sa'doun Hamadi. He told me he was very grateful for the fact that I had come not for political reasons but for humane reasons, for the sake of the children of Iraq. And he said, "We will show you everything and hide nothing. After seeing everything with your own eyes, please describe what you saw honestly to the Japanese people so they can judge the situation for themselves. For Iraq would like to have their reaction in addition to that of various other countries."

He said we could go anywhere and take any pictures we liked. And that is the way it was. There was no censorship or obstruction whatsoever.

Pinpoint Bombing

We next set off for Basra, 375 miles to the south of Baghdad, where we had been told there was serious malnutrition among the children. We drove for eight hours and, on the way, passed many army vehicles. We had heard that the previous day, government forces had clashed with the Kurds up in the north and that there had been five hundred casualties. I wondered, with misgivings, whether the army was hurrying north to suppress the conflict.

Most of the electric power pylons had been overturned by the bombing. It was shocking to see how the lethal accuracy of pinpoint bombing had done its work with some of the larger bridges. These were the bridges that carried communication cables and water pipes. It was palpable evidence of pinpoint bombing's terrifying capacity to pick out, in the dark, which bridges to target.

The blown-up bridges looked like ragged ghosts that had staggered forward and fallen flat on their faces into the Euphrates and other rivers. I had seen similar scenes in war movies, but the real thing was terrible to behold. The scary thing was that the smaller bridges which carried no cables had not been bombed. This is how advanced modern warfare has become.

An air-raid shelter that we saw in Baghdad provided further proof. It had been constructed four years earlier, in 1987, at the time of the Iran-Iraq War. It comprised a ground floor and a basement, each with an area of about five thousand square feet. The walls and ceilings had been blackened by the bombing, and the iron reinforcement rods jutted out from the concrete. It was dark inside except for a bright light that shone down in the middle of the room. This was a bombed-out hole in the ceiling. Two missiles, fired consecutively, had come through the hole. The first, like an awl, screwed open a hole in the thick concrete, while the second followed in with perfect precision and killed the occupants. According to the Iraqi defense ministry, all four hundred people in that shelter were killed. Half of them were children. What must the people have thought as they died, having confidently taken refuge there? The allies released a statement to the effect that they believed it was a building used by the army and hadn't known it was an air-raid shelter. But be that as it may, it is a fact that a lot of children were killed there. This is another clear example of how terrifying pinpoint bombing is.

As we approached Basra, we saw many more army vehicles. Basra is near Iraq's border with Kuwait. Since the end of the Gulf War, it has been a center of increasing antigovernment activity, thereby provoking government forces to mount keen vigilance there.

Basra, once called the Venice of the Middle East, and traditionally known as the place from which Sinbad set out to navigate the seven seas, was almost annihilated in the bombing during the Gulf War. The large power station outside Basra sustained thirteen attacks and was completely destroyed. It had been built by a Japanese enterprise thirteen years earlier. It produced 250,000 kilowatts and supplied electric power to a million people in the Basra area. Now it is just a gigantic piece of rubbish. The way it was destroyed precluded any possiblity of repair. What was once a power plant had become a lump of iron.

Since the supply of electric power had completely stopped, here, too, there was no way to purify the drinking water, no garbage disposal and no agricultural irrigation. There was no air conditioning in hospitals and no possibility whatsoever of performing operations. Similar conditions were prevalent throughout the country.

The Iraqi gentleman who showed us around the power plant told us he had worked there right from the time it was built. He said it was like his own child. To see it in ruins made him want to cry.

Ninety percent of Iraq's power stations were similarly destroyed. I know there were many reasons for doing so, but I couldn't help thinking how many children's lives would have been saved had this not been the case, and how many mothers' tears. I will keep on saying it: war is truly a cruel thing.

The Agony of Mothers

As we entered Basra, there was the same frightful smell of overflowing sewage as in Baghdad. Apparently, the effluent had gone down to some extent and was not the virtual lake it had been. Public health and sanitation experts were worried epidemics of infectious diseases such as cholera and typhoid fever might break out.

Children were playing happily, but the danger was already at their feet.

The water was cut off. Water rations were being supplied just as we were visiting, and water wagons were making the rounds. The water was cloudy, yet the children were drinking it with relish.

Nutritional conditions were bad and life was precarious. The children, nevertheless, watched us, their eyes brimming with curiosity. There is something so truly delightful about children. And it is always children like these who are the victims of war.

At the hospital attached to Basra University, we were first shown around the intensive care unit. The windowpanes had been shattered and beds thrown into disarray by the blast from a bomb that had fallen nearby. The oxygen inhalers were damaged and could not be used. The surgical instruments as well had been smashed. Several patients had died. Outside the window, we could see the hole made by the bomb. It was as big as a lake. The bomb hadn't even been dropped on the hospital. It was horrifying to think that all that damage was done simply by the secondary effects of the blast.

The examination and treatment of children at the hospital had recommenced, following a month-long suspension because of the bombing. There was no electricity, however. None of the hospitals could handle emergencies such as heart operations and kidney dialysis. The use of incubators for premature babies had already been impossible for some time.

A boy of nine with typhoid fever and a very high temperature lay in his bed just staring at the ceiling, in the saunalike heat. Medication to alleviate his fever was unavailable.

Conditions were the same at the health center in Adele. A child suffering from malnutrition lay limply in the arms of her mother, who kept crying all the while, "Please give me some milk, please give me some milk!"

There was a twelve-month-old baby, who still could not hold her head steady without wobbling; a baby who had been fed nothing but water and thin rice gruel for the past six or seven months, because there was no powdered milk; a baby nine months old, whose weight was still that of a three-month-old infant.

Two hundred children like that were brought to the health center each day.

I know about the agony of mothers in wartime when there is nothing. It is hard on the children, but harder on the mothers. It was probably the children's agony that prematurely aged these mothers, who were only about thirty-five or thirty-six, making them look like old women.

A young doctor shouted toward the camera, "I hope you will understand that there is nothing more painful for a doctor than not being able to treat his patients because of a lack of medicine and medical supplies." This echoed the words of the doctor in Baghdad.

I could only empathize with the doctors, both there and in in the capital.

IRAQ, 1991

Children as Land Mine Detectors

We traveled 220 miles north of Baghdad to Erbil, a town situated in the center of an area inhabited by the Kurds. It was about a ninety-minute flight by helicopter. Erbil had been the scene of a rebellion immediately after the Gulf War. It had been like a ghost town for some time after. The Kurds fled across the border to Iran, where they became refugees. Out of a million refugees, eight hundred thousand had returned, with apprehension. They had almost no provisions or water and were barely managing to survive.

We drove seventy-five miles to a Kurd refugee camp, some thirty-five miles from the Iranian border. There, two hundred thousand Kurdish refugees were living in tents under the blazing sun. They had no idea when they would be able to return to their homes. There was no prospect of peace negotiations. They said they were staying near the border so they could flee into Iran in case of an attack by Iraq's Saddam Hussein.

Although the heat then, in July, registered 122 degrees we were told it would be snowing in three months' time, come October. I wondered how they could possibly go through the winter in those tents. They were not even sturdy tents; they looked like chicken coops with scraps of cloth and bits of blanket laid over them.

The children were all barefoot and, of course, nutritionally deficient. But like children everywhere, they immediately came over and made friends with us. When I said *"Konnichi wa"* ("How do you do?") in Japanese, they copied me and said *"Konnichi wa"* back.

I had seen on TV the tragic sight of these several hundred thousand Kurdish refugees fleeing to Iran through the rain, taking with them nothing but the clothes on their backs, leading their children by the hand. Little kids were being dragged along in the fleeing columns, lots of them dying en route. It is tough on the children. I remember how it was as a child in wartime Japan. If your parents said walk, you walked, without a word. If my parents had told me to walk in another direction, without them, even I, who would normally have asked "Why?" would have obediently done as they said.

There were many land mines on the Iran-Iraq border left over from the war between the two countries. Someone told me, though I can't remember who (nor do I know whether or not the story is true), that people without land mine detectors would get orphan children to walk ahead of them. The child would be killed, of course, if he or she stepped on a mine, but the adults could follow safely. They would persuade orphans to do this by making the children, in their innocence, feel proud of walking ahead to test the ground.

The Soul of a Kurd

The refugee camp, too, was full of mothers' voices crying out, "Please give us milk, please give us water!"

Snow would be falling on the camp in a few months' time. They said 170,000 children would die within the half-year.

The huge sum of money Japan contributed to the allied war effort, if put toward other uses, would have saved the lives of seven million children—half of the fourteen million children on this earth who die each year —and provided a proper environment for them to grow up in. The money that vanished into thin air with those missiles could have given the children a future.

As we were about to leave the refugee camp, and were waving good-bye to the children, an elderly Kurdish man ran over and handed me something through the car window.

It was a small, decorated, antique knife.

The old man struggled to regain his breath as he explained, "We are a proud people. This knife is my soul, the soul of the Kurdish people. But I give it to you, to you who are working for the children."

I looked at the old man's face. It was sunburned and very wrinkled. His clothes were in tatters. He was of small stature and thin, yet there was something about him that was resolute and brave. There used to be old men like that in Japan.

I handed the knife back to him.

"I appreciate your thought. I accept that gratefully. But as for this knife, I wouldn't be allowed to take it into Japan. So please keep it for me. It makes me happy that you wanted to give me something as precious as that. I promise you that I'll go on working for the children."

As the car sped away, I could see the old man standing there in the dust. "I promise! I promise!" I kept repeating to myself, over and over.

CHAPTER NINE

ETHIOPIA, 1992

IN 1984, WHEN I FIRST MADE MY ACQUAINTANCE with real starvation, in Tanzania, Africa was being visited by a calamitous drought. Ethiopia, situated on what is known as "the Horn of Africa," was also suffering greatly. Every day we saw starving children on TV.

Eight years later, when it was arranged that I should visit Ethiopia toward the end of July 1992, I expected things to be a little better. The civil war had ended the year before, and Ethiopia was at peace. But I was mistaken. The war that had dragged on for thirty years and the drought that followed it had left the country terribly impoverished.

Ethiopia was overflowing with refugees. The people were without homes, without work, without food. I had the impression that the whole of Addis Ababa, the capital, was one gigantic refugee camp.

Refugees from Somalia

We first flew south from Addis Ababa for three hours to Dolo Odo, a village in the Borena region near the border with Somalia. Refugees continued to pour into that part of Ethiopia, escaping from the violent fighting going on in neighboring Somalia.

Only eighteen months earlier, Dolo Odo had been a small village with 3,500 inhabitants. Just as Ethiopia thought its own civil war was over, refugees from Somalia began coming in. Before too long, the population had swollen to seventy-two thousand. This figure was increasing daily.

It was depressing to find not a single tree there, nothing but reddish brown earth. It was the worst drought of the twentieth century. No rain had fallen for three years. Everything was bone dry. It was hot, and a strong wind kept blowing.

In an arid, desert-like place, I could see little earth mounds stretching off into the distance. They were the graves of the children who had died there. None of the graves had a marker bearing the child's name. There was no wood. The carcasses of animals that had died for lack of grass and water were scattered about. It seemed to me like the edge of the world.

The refugees lived in shelters resembling birdcages, made of tree branches, with withered grass and rags laid on top. A six-by-twelve-foot shelter would accommodate five or six people. It was hard to see how anyone could endure the hot sun and the cold nights in these flimsy dwellings. But it was better than nothing. There were no branches left. Many people were just squatting in the desert without any form of shelter. It was an awful situation.

I spoke to a young mother who was just crouching there crying incessantly. She was thin, and the skin around her eyes and lips was a mass of cracks.

"I'm hungry," she said, in a rasping voice that was barely audible.

"How long is it since you had a decent meal?" I asked.

"Eight months," she replied.

I was told that half of all the children in Dolo Odo died of starvation before reaching the age of five.

The wide Genae River, six miles south of the village, formed the natural boundary with Somalia. We went there. As we watched from the Ethiopian side, we saw raft after raft of people with their children coming across the river. The raftsmen expected a fee for their troubles. The opposite bank was crowded with people without the money to pay for the crossing. Over 150 people fleeing from Somalia arrived every day, I was told. They had no baggage or anything, only the clothes on their backs. At the most, a family might

ETHIOPIA, 1992

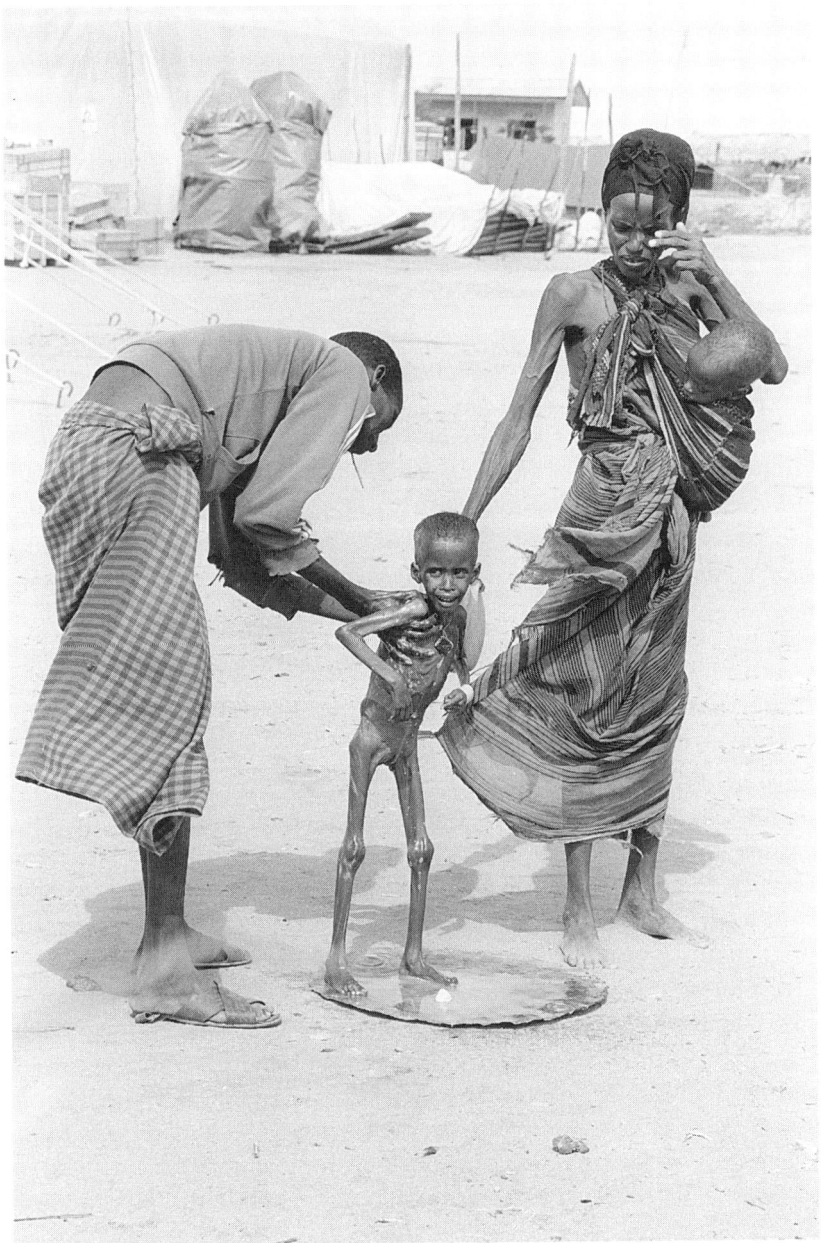

I had never seen a child as thin as this, walking with such desperate intent.

have a single bowl or a gourd for holding water.

I asked one of the refugees why they wanted to come over here. "Because we've heard there is food" was the reply. But there was a shortage of everything in Ethiopia, including food and water.

The children were all so thin. Though I had seen lots of thin children, it was the first time I had ever seen children so thin that their bones were plainly visible, yet they were not lying down but walking. They wore almost nothing, so you could see all the bones in their bodies.

Both the children fleeing from Somalia and the Ethiopian children were all thin. It was like watching a parade of skeletons. Not only were these children's ribs and hip bones visible, but their kneecaps were showing, too. I never knew before that there are two little round bones on either side of the kneecap. The children had lost all their hair, too, and I could clearly see the outline of their skulls. Nonetheless, they never lost heart or cried. They just kept on walking, keeping up with the adults. I was left speechless.

Paper Bracelets

It tore my heart apart to see the children in the weighing tent. That's where they decided who could receive food rations. There were so many refugees that there was not enough food to go around. The children would be weighed in the tent and if they were less than seventy percent of the weight they ought to be according to age and height, they would receive something to eat. For instance, if a baby who should weigh eleven pounds weighed under eight, it would be given rations. A woman who weighed 110 pounds would get nothing, but if her weight dropped to below seventy-five pounds, she would be entitled to some food. Children need food much, much more than adults, otherwise, their brains won't develop. Their blood vessels, internal organs, and everything else also require food when the children are small to start developing.

The scales were not the kind that you stand on. They were a much sturdier type, the ones that you hang from. Step-on scales would probably break with so many people standing on them. Small children and babies were hung in a cloth bag from the scales. Children over three had to hang on themselves. All the children looked even thinner as they hung with their arms from the scales. Their bones were more visible, too. I had never seen anything so tragic.

When I think of all of us in Japan going on diets and trying like mad to lose weight! Half the advertisements in women's magazines are selling ways to get thin. And here were these children who were all so desperately skinny, and yet if they were even as little as three or four ounces over the seventy percent threshold they would be given nothing. The people doling out the rations would have liked to give food to all the children. Food supplies were limited because they had to be transported by air and there was never enough to go around. The children quietly waited their turn to be weighed. When I thought of the abundance of food in Japan, I wanted to cry.

Children who were thirty percent below normal weight were given paper bracelets and sent to the next tent to receive their ration. The food being doled out was hardly tasty; it was simply a mixture of wheat flour, corn flour and soy flour boiled into a thin gruel with river water.

The children squatted down and greedily gulped the gruel from orange-colored plastic containers. Small as they were, the instinct for survival was strong. I couldn't bear to think of those children whose weight might have risen a wee bit above the seventy percent by the next day, thus causing them to be denied their ration.

Starved of Love, Too

Many of the children in the weighing tent were suffering from dehydration caused by diarrhea. They were so emaciated they looked as if they were dying. Their skin just hung on them and was terribly wrinkled—not small wrinkles, but big, twisted folds of skin. They looked like the children I saw in Bangladesh. They were given oral rehydration salts—a mixture of sugar and salt dissolved in water. Children too weak to drink had the solution dripped into their mouths by a helper with a syringe.

There was a little girl of about two and a half among this group.

ETHIOPIA, 1992

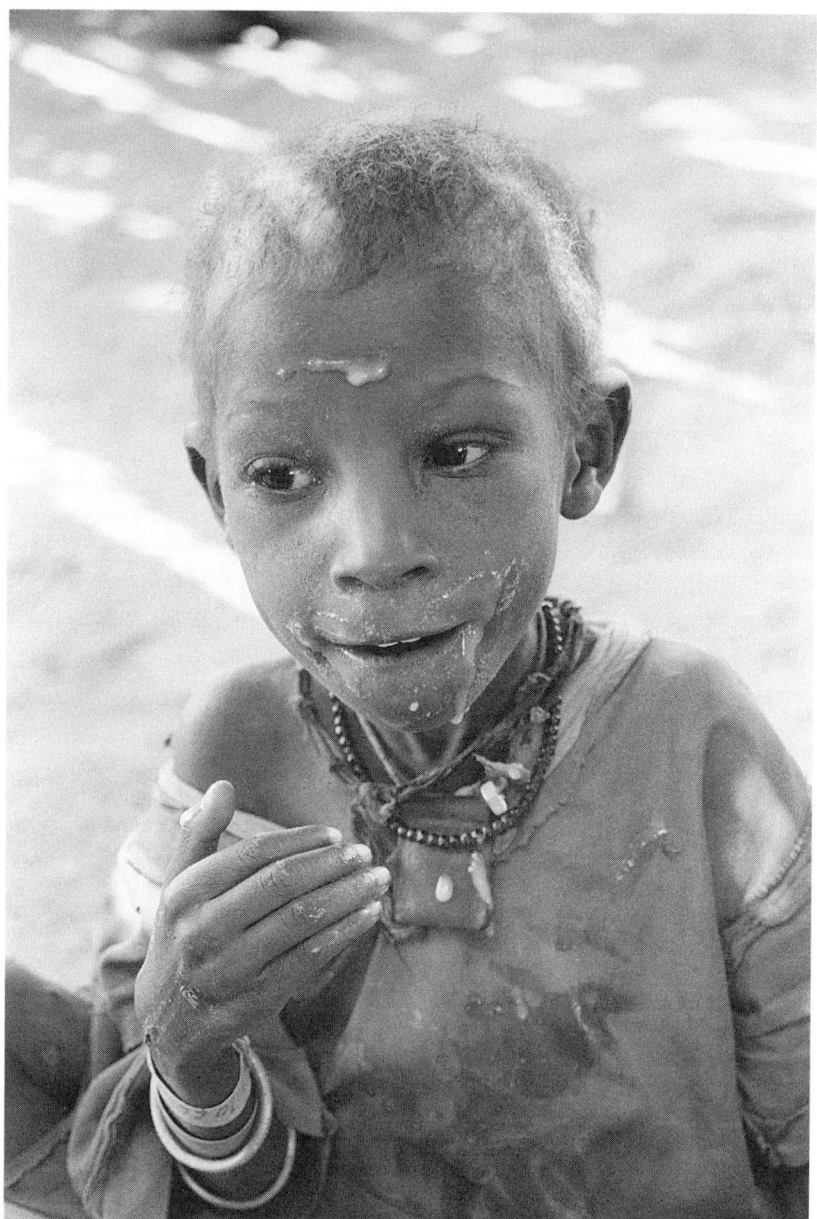

A very happy child who was given a paper bracelet that entitled him to a food ration. The thinness and loss of hair are signs of malnutrition.

ETHIOPIA, 1992

She was leaning against the wall of the tent, completely naked. By her feet was a puddle she had made with her diarrhea. An adult with a plastic tumbler of oral salt solution was trying to get her to drink from it. The child took hold of the tumbler and emptied its contents on the ground. She was probably in pain, and I sympathized with her for fretting. She was an orphan, I discovered.

If she did not drink, she would die of dehydration. The volunteer tried again and again, but each time the child threw the tumbler away.

I thought I would see if I could get her to drink from the tumbler. I squatted down beside her. "Now then, dear, you must drink this, you know. If you do you'll get better. That's a good girl! Drink it and see." I handed her the tumbler. Looking up at me, she drank it all. I gave her another tumblerful, and she drank that too.

I was choked with emotion. What that child needed was not medicine or food, but a gentle word. If I could have stayed with her every day, I'm sure she would have recovered. But I obviously couldn't. I picked up that feces-smeared child in my arms and said to her as gently as I could, "Are you all right now? Promise me you'll be a good girl and drink whatever they want you to. Then you'll get well and grow big and strong. Promise me that, won't you?"

She listened to me intently and looked right into my eyes. She probably had no idea what I was saying, but I'm quite sure she understood that someone was speaking to her kindly.

These were wartime conditions, and the people looking after the refugees did not have time to dispense comfort and cheer. Even at the clinic, they were so inundated with dying children, there was no time for tender words. One realized that. But all the same, it was pitiful. I am convinced that for children to be starved of love is as bad as their being starved of food. Everyone needs love.

Why Is Everybody Looking at Me?

At the clinic in Dolo Odo, there were four volunteers, including a Dutch lady doctor from Belgium's NGO *Médecins sans frontières* and an English nurse.

ETHIOPIA, 1992

Even in the vicinity of the clinic, fifteen to twenty children were dying every day. The Dutch doctor said that many mothers did not bring their children to the clinic even if they were ill. Or, by the time they did, it was usually too late.

There was a one-year-old baby there whose mother had been brave enough to bring her in. Her breathing was wheezy and made a grating sound. The doctor said she was dying. She only weighed seven pounds. In Japan, that is usually what babies weigh at birth. She was tiny and so thin her skull was visible. The doctor pinched her skin and it stayed pinched.

A nine-year-old girl had extreme malnutrition and dehydration. She was minus the toes of her left foot, having been scalded as an infant. Her face was thin, with prominent cheekbones, which made her look like a mummy.

All of a sudden, the girl said, "Why is everybody looking at me?"

I admit I was staring at her too, and the TV camera was pointed at her, although the lights were not on. I was flustered but managed to reply, "It's because you're so pretty."

The girl tried her best to smile. Pitifully, her face did not resemble a smiling child's at all. Yet you could clearly tell that she was smiling from her heart.

Children are sincere and pure. I hadn't told a complete lie, but my heart ached to think that it was not because I thought the girl was pretty that I'd originally been looking at her. To this day I can see in my mind that girl's face as she tried hard to smile. Because of that smile, I made a vow to try never, ever to hurt the feelings of a pure, innocent child.

In the countries of Africa and Asia that I visited, I had met countless children suffering from malnutrition. Ethiopia was the first place where I had seen so many children who were so thin—almost skeletal—all walking along obediently with their parents.

After all, such conditions were nothing new to the Ethiopians. They had already known thirty years of civil war and been assailed by a series of droughts. When I thought of those mothers and their children and all the tears they must have shed during the past three decades, I was abashed and saddened at my ignorance and lack of action.

No More Jungle Anywhere

There were no wells in Dolo Odo.

The river water stored in oil drums was muddy and brown. There was no kindling to make a fire in order to boil it. This was the sort of muddy water even the sick children were drinking, straight from the drums. Consequently, children got upset stomachs, and sick children became sicker.

There were no trees in the northern Tigray region, either. Nothing but open plain as far as the eye could see. It seemed peaceful enough, but it was really just denuded earth without a single farm of any sort. Even the distant hills were treeless and bare.

The Ethiopian representative from UNICEF who was taking us around, a man in his forties, told us there had been lots of trees there when he was a boy.

Originally, Ethiopia had been covered in forest, but now only three percent remained. As for jungle, there was none left anywhere.

It is easy enough to say it would have been better not to cut down the trees. But in Tigray there is no electricity or gas. The people had to cut down the trees in order to cook their food and keep warm through the cold nights.

To make rain, there must be enough trees and vegetation to absorb the rain. This then evaporates and becomes cloud, which again produces rain. As mentioned in the chapter on Niger, this full cycle is essential.

Ethiopia was determined to increase the number of trees and was making efforts toward reforestation. They were using more or less the same methods as those used in the Niger desert. Here, they planted seeds in earth-filled plastic tubes. These were watered and, when the saplings had grown to about twelve inches, they were taken to the hills and transplanted.

Planting saplings on all the hills of Ethiopia would be no easy task. Water would have to be taken there too. The very thought of it was enough to make one faint. Nevertheless, there was no other way to improve the environment and bring rain.

I planted a tree. There is an Ethiopian tree called a *Kundo berbere*, which is remarkably suited to the country. Firstly, it grows fast; secondly, it does not need much water; and thirdly, animals, both wild and domestic, dislike the taste and will not touch it. This is important, since domestic animals have caused the disappearance of many plants by eating them. Fourthly, when the *Kundo berbere* is full grown, it provides very hard wood, ideal for building. Near the tree I planted, they put up a tiny sign with my name on it. I hoped the tree would grow well.

The population of the Tigray region was 4.8 million. Incidentally, the population of the whole of Ethiopia this same year (1992) was 50,400,000. This figure might not be accurate because of the refugees who were traveling back and forth across the border.

The Tigray region was home to many of the people who opposed the dictatorial regime of former president Mengistu. For that reason, Tigray had sustained a concentrated attack. Half of its 546 schools were destroyed. One hundred thousand farmers from this region alone were killed in the fighting, forty thousand of them women—the mothers of the farming villages fighting the government. I have never experienced a civil war. Nevertheless, I could imagine the ravages brought on by thirty years of sustained warfare. As I stood before a monument inscribed "To the souls of the hundred thousand people who died fighting on this land," I thought how fortunate we were in my country to have lived in the midst of peace for almost fifty years.

We also went to a place called Kilisha Imini, which had been bombed by the former government forces in an effort to eliminate the guerrillas holed up there. Its name means "place where stones collect," and there certainly were lots of rocks and stones all over the place. Here, too, there was no sign of a tree as far as the eye could see.

The only clinic had been destroyed by bombing. Sick children had to be taken on foot along a rock-strewn mountain road to a town that had a doctor. However, this trip took at least a couple of hours, even by car. Going to a doctor was therefore out of the question for the village people. The general opinion was that sick children would just have to die.

Ethiopia is a high-altitude country. Its capital, Addis Ababa, is

7,875 feet above sea level. Kilisha Imini is even higher. The day we were there, it was raining and very cold.

There was a small school whose windows and ceiling had been blown away by the bombing. There were no chairs, desks or paper to write on—nothing. In spite of this, the children were sitting on the cold floor, busy doing their lessons. They were confidently reading passages aloud, trying out their new reading skills.

The Brown Whale

It happened on our way back along the rock-strewn road from Kilisha Imini. We were traveling in four Land Rovers. Just as the car ahead of us turned, I saw something quite incredible. I caught sight of it briefly on our right—something that looked like a huge, chocolate-brown whale. Before I had time to exclaim, "What was that?" a torrent of brown water suddenly came hurtling across our path with terrifying velocity just where the car in front of us had been a moment before. It was a flash flood.

In the twinkling of an eye, the water became a roaring, swirling river about fifty feet wide and over six feet deep. It was not like an ordinary swift current. If the car in front of us had passed the spot a second or two later, it would have been swept away for good.

I stared at the river as though I was seeing something in a nightmare and thought, "This is the sort of thing they mean when they report in the paper that people were killed in a flash flood in Ethiopia."

As I wondered what had caused it, I heard that the night before there had been rain in some far-off mountains. Because of the total lack of trees and the drought, the earth was rock hard. The water from the rain flowed down the side of the mountain like a cascade. Gathering more water on its way it shot across the parched earth like an arrow. Nature can be very frightening.

"Yes," said one of the Ethiopians, who did not seem very surprised, "this happens from time to time. The muddy water will subside in about an hour."

Our leading car arrived back on the opposite bank about an

hour later. They had just driven on without looking back. When they finally noticed we were not behind them, they got worried and returned to find that a river had appeared between us. We tried to converse by shouting across the river, but the noise of the torrent drowned out our voices. We were resigned to the fact that there was nothing we could do but wait for the water level to go down. Then we remembered that our lunches were packed in the leading car, over there on the opposite bank. It was well past lunch time. Naturally, we had no cellular or wireless phones. "We've just *got* to get in touch with them," I thought. And then I had a good idea.

Why not put a note and a stone in a plastic bag, close it tightly, and throw it over to the other side?

Someone who has spent his or her childhood playing all sorts of games is useful at times like this. First I got the young assistant cameraman on our side of the river to practice with just a stone in the bag. When we found it worked, I put in a note saying "What have you done with the lunch boxes?" and got him to throw that across. The message arrived there all right, and back came the reply, "Today's lunch is just biscuits. We'll send some over."

Nobody else had thought of sending messages back and forth like that. Very soon the plastic bag with the stone and some of the biscuits came flying over from the other bank, and all ended satisfactorily.

We ate our biscuits and waited for the water to subside. After three hours, it had finally sunk to knee depth. Quite a crowd of people, whose destinations lay somewhere on that road, had gradually gathered on either bank. Among them was an old woman with a donkey.

We knew the water had become knee-deep because a vigorous youth on the opposite bank gave a hearty yell and stepped in. It was shallow enough, but the current was strong. The youth felt his way carefully and slowly and made it over to our side. Just as I thought he was going to come up the bank, he turned and went

ETHIOPIA, 1992

This is the muddy river that appeared in the twinkling of an eye. That's me wandering about on the right on the opposite bank.

back. The old woman was a stranger, but he hoisted her on his back and brought her over to our side. As for the donkey, he urged it forward with a slap on its rump and a shove, and it came over safely, too, doing a sort of dog paddle. Thanks to the young man's traffic control, all the others—not counting us—managed to cross over.

    The chauffeur of my car was an excellent driver. "Let's go." he said. "I don't think the Land Rover will have any trouble with this amount of water. But hold on tight!" It was like the movies as we splashed across, swaying backward and forward. We got to the other side and climbed up the bank, finally stopping on a level place. The driver then got out, rolled up his trousers, and waded back across the river to the other bank where we had been. He probably thought the other two drivers would not be able to cope with the difficult crossing. All went well.

We were four hours behind schedule when we finally started for home.

If that water had not gone down sufficiently, we would have had to spend the night in the wilderness, since there was no other road. I think it would have been a terrible night, and very cold. What I thought was a chocolate-brown whale must have been the flash flood shooting up at some point. Little did I know what a fearsome thing that "whale" would turn out to be.

Alleluia

We got into an airplane again and flew for three hours up north to Bahir Dar, in the Gojiam region.

We visited the market in Bahir Dar, which was held every Saturday. There were fruits and vegetables and other things. The most valuable item was firewood. Without firewood, grains were impossible to eat.

I asked a woman who was nursing her baby at the side of the road, with firewood spread out on the ground beside her, how far she had walked to find the wood.

"Twenty miles," she replied.

All that distance to collect only the amount of firewood she could carry on her head, with her baby on her back.

"How long do you have to search to collect that amount of wood?"

"It takes me eleven hours."

That was how few trees were left in Ethiopia.

After walking under the blazing sun along twenty miles of rock-strewn roads, with the firewood on her head and her baby on her back, even if she sold it all, it would only bring her two or three dollars. The buyers were poor, too, so it was not easy to sell. She would have to carry home what firewood was left. The firewood vendors were all women. So many of the men had been killed in the civil war.

ETHIOPIA, 1992

In 1991, the year the war ended, the population of the capital, Addis Ababa, increased by one million. Many who had fled returned, and people from other countries flocked in. The city's population of 650,000, only five years earlier, had increased to 3.4 million, seventy percent of whom were living below the poverty line.

We visited the area where Addis Ababa University was. All along the walls of the university were tents of plastic sheeting, which served as housing for refugees. There were wounded soldiers and amputees from the civil war, as well as war widows.

I looked inside one of the tents. It was about nine feet by six. "There are fifteen of us," said the mother. "We don't know what we'll do next."

There are said to be one hundred thousand street children—homeless children and orphans—begging and selling things on the streets of Ethiopian towns. If parents cannot look after their children, the children have to go out and fend for themselves.

I gathered a group of these children together and sang Mozart's *Alleluia* to them. Whenever I do that in my little birdlike soprano, children are delighted and join in. It is easy, with all its repeated alleluias, and they learn it quickly. As we sang it together, holding hands, I suddenly thought how delighted Mozart would have been!

After saying good-bye to the children, we got in the car and set off for an orphanage, our next scheduled visit. Soon after we arrived there and were being taken on an inspection tour, a little girl came over to me and pulled my slacks. Just as I was wondering what she wanted, she said "Alleluia" in a tiny voice, as if it were a secret code between us.

The girl must have been one of those street children, although the orphanage was quite a distance away from where we had been. Could she have followed our cars and run all that way? She was so sweet, and yet so pitiable. I felt like weeping.

I Want to Be Alive

When we were met at the airport in Ethiopa, a fourteen-year-old girl handed me a bouquet. Her name was Selamawit. She had been

ETHIOPIA, 1992

a street child. At the age of five, she had been asked by a UNICEF photographer what she wanted to be when she grew up, to which she had replied, "I want to be alive."

When asked that question, girls usually say things like, "I want to be a stewardess," or "I want to get married." A close-up of that girl's face, with those words, was made into a UNICEF poster. Her words seemed to typify all the children and the situation they were in.

Selawamit had fortunately lived to the age of fourteen. I was able to ask her the same question she had been asked nine years earlier. She smiled, and this time she said, "I want to be a doctor and cure sick children."

Ministers and government officials I met told me that now that the country finally was at peace, they wanted to rebuild their devastated nation and firmly reestablish education and medical facilities.

But at that time, fifteen hundred children under the age of five were dying every day from diseases stemming from starvation. What was needed was food, medical supplies and safe drinking water.

We flew home to Japan via Rome. The airport in Rome was a completely different world. People were dressed well, conditions were hygienic, there was everything one could want in the way of food.

It takes much, much longer to get to Mozambique and Angola from Europe. But Ethiopia was only six hours away. In the desert, children were lining up that very day to be weighed, and tearful mothers were pleading for water and milk.

Somehow it felt even stranger to be back in Japan, living contentedly, wanting for nothing, with proper water, any amount of food in the refrigerator and television to watch.

I kept saying to myself, "Dear God, isn't it a little unfair?"

Chapter Ten

SUDAN, 1993

It was to be my tenth expedition as a UNICEF goodwill ambassador. After consultation with UNICEF and others, it was decided that I should visit Africa's largest country, Sudan.

Sudan covers roughly one million square miles. It shares borders with nine countries: Egypt, Eritrea, Ethiopia, Kenya, Uganda, Zaire, the Central African Republic, Chad and Libya. In 1993, Sudan was a country saddled with serious problems: an intense civil war, a drought, and a population of twenty-five million, sixty percent of whom were dependent on various overseas aid programs as their only means of obtaining food and other daily essentials. Just think, only twenty-five people per square mile. I was astounded to learn that thirty percent of the land—roughly one third—was uninhabited desert.

From Japan, it took us a whole day to get to Khartoum, the capital.

As soon as we arrived, we attended a briefing session at UNICEF's office, where they informed us that we were to travel in "a light aircraft for more than 2,500 miles, then transfer to a car for a drive of over 300 miles." Few of the roads are surfaced in this huge country.

I met the minister for foreign affairs. He was also a brain surgeon. He said, "Regarding the civil war, I want it settled by negotiation rather than weapons, because the victims are always the children. You may photograph anywhere in any way you wish. We have nothing to hide. I want you to see my country as it is, with your own eyes."

It was winter, supposedly the best time to visit the Sudan. Even so, the midday temperature regularly rose into the hundreds. Without air conditioning it is practically impossible to work in this heat. Citizens of Khartoum start work early in the cool of the morning, and finish by two o'clock in the afternoon.

Like them, we, too, began our day at five or six o'clock in the morning.

Soccer Balls

Few Sudanese households had plumbing or running water even in Khartoum. The people spent up to half their income on water, purchased from the very many water vendors who plied their trade from oil drums off the back of donkey-drawn carts. It was difficult to imagine having to spend such a high proportion of one's earnings on something like water, which I had always taken for granted.

UNICEF's policy of supplying water was being actively pursued here in Khartoum, too. Since 1991, over two hundred wells had been dug around the seventy-thousand-strong refugee camp in Jebel Awlia, a town located twenty-five miles south of Khartoum.

There were thirty-five such camps around Khartoum alone, accommodating a total of 710,000 refugees. That is almost a quarter of Khartoum's original population of 3.3 million people. Imagine three million refugees living in a suburb twenty-five miles from the center of Tokyo, New York or London.

The people in the camps lived in windowless mud huts, which became as hot as a roasting pot inside and were reduced to mud whenever it rained. Most of the refugees had lost their families in the civil war or to the drought. Their homes, too, had been lost when they left their farms and fled to safety.

An old man representing the residents was said to have led eleven thousand villagers in their flight. He told me that more than four thousand had died during the exodus. He said most of his children were dead, as was his wife.

Grief was etched into his face with his wrinkles. He ended by saying, "Now that there's peace, I would like to go back to my village. There is nothing to hope for here, except to get older and wait for death. But it's very far away, and my land has probably gone to rack and ruin. And the house is gone. So I guess there's nothing I can do."

The refugee camp had an occupational training center for women. People from the German government's international development agency were giving training courses in dyeing, sewing and soap making. Women in the sewing class had learned to make eight blouses or four suits in a week. They were making money by selling these.

We visited a class in health education at the elementary school in the Jebel Awlia refugee camp.

We asked the children what they wanted most right now. "I want to study more," "I want to learn things that are more advanced," "I want a notebook," were some of the replies.

In the midst of the clamor, I heard one tiny voice say, "A soccer ball." I was surprised to learn that there were more than a hundred soccer teams in the camp. After all, there were seventy thousand people there. When we went to see what sort of balls the teams were using, we found they were just made of rolled-up old rags, nothing like the nice balls that Japanese children kick around.

Nevertheless, although the children were undernourished and had no proper balls, they were running around for all they were worth.

"I must see that they get some soccer balls," I thought. How nice they would look, shiny new black-and-white soccer balls flying through the Sudanese sky!

Peace One

The central Kordofan region of Sudan is an area that has very little rain, and that only between June and September. UNICEF was digging a well in Casseba, a relatively large village with a population of fifteen hundred.

Until then, the inhabitants of the area would get their water by either eating wild watermelons, ladling water from puddles left during the rainy season, and seeing what they could find in the cavities of the enormous baobab tree trunks. Baobabs are sometimes called "topsy-turvy trees" because they are funny-looking trees that seem to be upside down, with their roots pointing up to the sky. Saint-Exupéry mentions them in *The Little Prince*. Big ones can grow to sixty feet, with trunks thirty feet in diameter.

Excavators for digging wells are extremely expensive. One costs about five hundred thousand dollars; however, a well can be dug here for about three thousand dollars, saving fifteen hundred people from spending the whole day walking to a river to get water.

We next visited a town in the Upper Nile region, in the south of Sudan, called Nasir. This area was controlled by the antigovernment Sudan People's Liberation Army. Intense fighting between the SPLA and government forces meant that our official escorts from Khartoum could not stay safely in the region and so returned to the capital.

Over a thousand people were waiting to greet us, as our small aircraft landed. The adults performed a dance while the children welcomed us by clapping as hard as they could.

The children's clothes were in tatters and their hair covered in mud and dust. They were skinny. Many of the children were naked. No one was wearing shoes.

The children all held pieces of paper in their hands, each with a different message: "Peace One," "Training our teachers," "School uniform," "School materials." It was like being surrounded by a petition group. The desire for peace was obviously shared by them all. There had been a bomb attack only two days earlier.

Most of the people had lost their homes and families in the civil war. In spite of that, the children smiled and were friendly, and held out their hands to me. One small child pushed its hand through a gap in the crowd. "Why, fancy seeing you here," I said as I squeezed it.

The children were like angels. They seemed to have no idea who were friends and who were enemies, or even what had happened to their parents. They had no idea how they looked, either. All they knew was that they were there by the skin of their teeth and were pleased to be shaking my hand.

SUDAN, 1993

I Want to Go to School

The southern part of Sudan was in particular need of emergency aid. With the cooperation of various United Nations agencies, such as the World Food Program, UNICEF was sending food and medical supplies to Sudan as part of an operation called Operation Lifeline Sudan. We saw some of those relief goods being unloaded in Nasir.

Nevertheless, supplies were strictly limited, barely enough to allow the people one meal a day. Among the relief goods were biscuits. We noticed that they were from the government of Japan.

Shipping the biscuits to the Sudan was not at all easy. From Japan, the biscuits went first by sea to the Kenyan port of Mombasa, a voyage that takes a good many days; after which they were delivered overland by truck to somewhere near the Kenya–Sudan border. This added a further three or four days to the schedule. Furtive guerrilla activities in the region made road haulage too risky. The biscuits had to be flown to Nasir. The flight takes a couple of hours.

Shipping costs were many times greater than the cost of the actual relief goods themselves. What a waste! What a mess war made!

There was a river near where the relief goods were being unloaded. It was the color of *café au lait*. The children were in it up to their waists, drinking the water with relish.

Although it was heartbreaking to see those innocent children drinking the water, my instinct was that it would have been wrong to have undermined their ignorance. And yet the small children were bound to get diarrhea from drinking river water, and then the other diseases that invariably follow, many of them infectious. How many children must have lost their lives in just this way? But there was no other drinking water here and no firewood with which to boil it. Mothers with babes in arms were in the river, too, scooping up the water with their hands for their infants.

The civil war in Sudan had been going on for a long time, the past ten years being particularly severe. About three hundred thousand people had fled to neighboring Ethiopia and other countries. Ethiopia's military regime having been toppled in 1991, there was a new regime there now. Fearing persecution, the Sudanese refugees had gone back to their homeland, despite the hostilities still going on.

SUDAN, 1993

Children drinking muddy river water. Unhygienic though it was, there was no other drinking water to be had.

The Ketbak camp in Nasir catered for sixteen hundred orphans who had become separated from their families in the civil war. Their parents had died, and they were without relatives. The camp was like a wasteland. The children did not even have a proper place to sleep. Few of the orphans wore clothes; most ran around naked. There was no food or writing materials, nor any building that could be used as a school. But the children all pleaded to go to school and study. They wanted this as earnestly as the adults wanted food and medical supplies.

I had met lots of children as a UNICEF goodwill ambassador. This was the first time I had come across children so eager to study.

The local UNICEF people said the children probably thought they would find something nice at school and that it would remind them of what it was like to be part of a family.

We left the area that was under the control of the SPLA and headed toward Juba, Sudan's southernmost city and still governed from Khartoum. South of that was, again, rebel country. The civil war had created a complicated situation in Sudan. Juba itself had been the scene of repeated clashes between the warring parties. Out of a population of 400,000, 240,000 were dependent on emergency aid for basic survival, even right after the harvest. For the rest of the year, all 400,000 Jubans depended on the supplies that were dropped by air.

Vendors were setting up their stalls at Konyokony market, Juba's largest. It reminded me of Japan's black market right after the end of the war.

I had heard about the ten thousand street children at the market. They were like black-market waifs: they were orphans wandering about the market with their friends, looking for something interesting to happen. These children had no accommodation and received no aid.

There were fourteen refugee camps around Juba, where about seventy thousand people lived. There was a shortage of everything. For example, the main cause of children's deaths in Sudan was malaria, yet there was no more malaria medicine left anywhere. In Jebel Kujur camp, where thirteen thousand people lived, seventy-five percent were undernourished.

At the orphanage, there were children whose parents had been killed in the civil war or had died of disease, as well as children who had been abandoned by mothers too young to raise them. There was a particularly large number of very small children, not much beyond the infant stage.

"We'd like to give the babies nourishing milk," said the director, "but there is none, so we are feeding them boiled beans."

Bitten on the Head by Hyenas

We flew to Lokichokio, a town situated only fifteen miles from the Kenyan border. Our small aircraft took care to avoid the area where opposing factions of the SPLA were fighting each other. Monthly airlifts of six thousand tons of aid foodstuffs were being made from an Operation Lifeline Sudan base near the town. Twenty-nine international NGOs and two Sudanese NGOs were based there.

We visited a Red Cross hospital. It had 320 beds, an operating theater, a general surgery department and an orthopedic department. From the outside, it looked like a field hospital; inside, it was the real thing. There was even a rehabilitation ward.

Most of the patients were either suffering from gunshot wounds or had lost legs when they stepped on a land mine. I had visited a great many places in Sudan. This place, in particular, brought home to me the tragedy of civil war.

There was a ten-year-old boy in one of the wards who had lost a leg. "I was in some bushes," he said, "and someone suddenly shot at me." The wound had festered, and they were forced to amputate.

"Was the man who shot you in uniform?" I asked.

"No, he was dressed in ordinary clothes."

The war in Sudan was between government and antigovernment forces. The latter had recently divided into two factions and were fighting each other. How could children tell who was an enemy and who was a friend? If someone suddenly shot at you from a bush, all you could do was run for your life! Small children invariably failed to get away in time.

There were lots of children who had been shot: children who

had had their brains blown out and were left as human vegetables, those who were left half paralyzed, and others who, having been shot in the legs, had shattered bones.

A nurse was giving a piggyback ride to a four-year-old boy with a bandaged leg. He was crying. The bullet had passed through his leg between the small bones without fracturing them. He had been lucky.

The children who had been brought to the hospital were the lucky ones. The hospital was well equipped and could cope with any sort of operation or treatment.

Nervertheless, it was dreadful to think of small children like this being shot at, and from behind, too.

There were doctors and nurses from many different countries working hard there. Among them was a twenty-nine-year-old nurse from Japan. Masako Kawamura had been sent from the Nagoya No. 1 Red Cross Hospital. She had been in Lokichokio for three months. A pretty nurse with a beaming smile, she said, "Even the ones who have lost their legs say that when they're well, they want to fight again for their country, even if they have to do it in a wheelchair. I can't bear to hear them say things like that."

There were a lot of children in the hospital who had been bitten on the head by hyenas. Although I had been to Africa many times, until then I had not heard anyone mention anything about wild animals. There was a boy of seven or eight whose head and legs were in bandages. The bite to his head had been particularly vicious, and a skin graft had been necessary. Hence those bandages on his legs.

I was shown the scar on the head of a child whose bandages had already been removed. I could still see the row of tooth marks the hyena made when it snapped its huge jaw down on the poor child's head. Besides the pain of being bitten, there's the terror and the scarred psyche. I don't think any of us can even imagine what it must be like. I was told that many of the children die when the wound is left to fester.

Hyena bites may not have any direct connection with the civil war, but if there had been no war, the villages would not have been attacked, the children would not have lost their families and their homes, and they would not be sleeping by themselves, curled up on the ground, without shelter.

There was a thirteen-year-old boy who was bandaged all the way down from his right eye to his arm. He had been walking along when a land mine exploded in his path. A piece of it became lodged in his eye. In fact, he was to have the eyeball removed the next day, but he had not been told about the operation and did not know that he had lost the sight of that eye. He was devouring his maize gruel with obvious pleasure.

"What do you want to be when you grow up?" I asked him.

"I want to be a doctor and cure people's diseases," he replied, nonchalantly.

"You'll stick to that, won't you?" I said, trying as best I could to sound convincing.

His Mother's Breast

While I was going hither and yon visiting various wards in the hospital, a boy about five years old came and stood near me. His arm was in a sling. Perhaps he had been shot. All of a sudden, the boy grabbed my breast with his left hand. I was wearing a T-shirt. He stayed like that and didn't let go. Perhaps he was embarrassed, because his face was turned away from me. Or was he thinking of his mother? It's good, I thought, if that's a comfort to him, so I just stood there.

My skin color was different from that of his mother, and so was my face, and the language I spoke, and everything else. But none of that mattered to that child. He had been an orphan ever since he was small and had spent his life fleeing. Now he had been shot and brought to the hospital. He must have felt ever so lonely. In a country like that, children of five are treated as adults. I think he must have thought of his mother and wanted her so badly he couldn't contain himself and had to touch my breast.

The boy didn't move.

After about five minutes, I took his little hand away and crouched down in front of him and looked into his face. He was a boy with a

SUDAN, 1993

This boy, an orphan who had been shot at, suddenly touched my breast. He must have been thinking of his mother.

beautiful face and large eyes. I took his hand in mine and said, "Everything's going to be all right now, isn't it? You were thinking about your mother, weren't you? But you have had a good feel, and I think that's enough for now. So good luck, and God bless!"

The child had been looking at my eyes as I spoke, and when I finished, he nodded, just as if he had understood my Japanese.

What these children long for is the touch of a warm hand, kind words and a comforting female presence. I have learned that these things are as necessary to a child's well-being as medicine and food. Come to think of it, it was in order to cure wounded soldiers more quickly at the front that Florence Nightingale instigated a reform that changed rough hospital orderlies into white-robed "angels" with gentle hands.

Eighty-five Percent of the Children

Sudan is a country with a long history and a rich cultural heritage. The pyramids of Sudan may not be as old as those in Egypt, but during the eleven hundred years from 700 B.C.–A.D. 400 about seven hundred of these structures were built.

In the Meroe Desert, north of Khartoum, on the road to Egypt, there are still about fifty pyramids as well as palace ruins. Formerly the Kingdom of Meroe, the city used to be the most prosperous in the Sudan.

The sun, as it set in the desert there, was the biggest sun I have ever seen. "What beautiful sunsets they have in this country," I thought. But the people of Sudan were all so preoccupied, no one ever said anything like, "What a beautiful sunset."

Obviously, considering the situation the country was in, it was no time for carefree gazing at the setting sun. And yet, if the civil war had not still been going on, tourists would certainly have flocked to this history-steeped country.

On my return to Japan, the account of my travels in Sudan was broadcast on television. I received a letter from the Sudanese ambassador in Tokyo.

> I want to express my gratitude to you for your thoughtfulness toward the children of my country and the way you looked at our country from a humane standpoint, not discriminating between enemies and friends. Seeing you make physical contact with the children of our country brought tears to my eyes.

Sudan was a country with many problems, but for us there were neither friends nor enemies, only victims. We visited areas under the control of the government forces and others under the control of the rebels. To the children, too, there were neither friends nor enemies.

SUDAN, 1993

Ten years had passed since my visit to Tanzania, my first assignment as a UNICEF goodwill ambassador. I felt grateful to have been given such a task. If I had not had that opportunity, I would never have been able to make the acquaintance of all these children around the world.

At that time, eighty-five percent of the children on this planet were without good drinking water. They also lacked food for sufficient nourishment and were unable to receive inoculations. Having to work to help their families, these children could not study even if they wanted to. The children had become involved in civil wars and many became orphans. And with all that, they tried desperately to survive.

Eighty-five percent. Japan is a fortunate, industrialized nation. Japanese children are part of the remaining fifteen percent. I am not saying, "See how lucky they are compared with children like those in Sudan!" But when all is said and done, don't you really think our children have a better life than those who have lost their parents, sleep on the ground, and never know when they might be shot at from behind or bitten on the head by a hyena?

Chapter Eleven

RWANDA, 1994

Rwanda was once called the Switzerland of Africa.

Looking down at it from the sky, I could see tiers of fields stretching up to Rwanda's peaks. From here, at least, Rwanda looked a free and beautiful land, reminding me of my home land. The African landscapes I had seen so far had all been savage and brutal. Here, the land was fertile, and had there been no civil war, the people would no doubt be enjoying plentiful harvests.

When we landed at Kigali, the capital, I noticed first that the buildings were riddled with bullet holes. Airport security was rigorous because no one could know what might happen next. Evidence of the horrors of the recent war could be seen in the ruins of Kigali's buildings.

One million of the country's population of 7.5 million had been massacred.

Kigali had been completely deserted for some time, but gradually people were coming back from the places they had fled to. The open-air market in the city center had begun to regain some of its bustle, but sales of rice, maize, beans, soap and firewood were still a trickle. Customers were scarce, and money was in short supply. When the people connected with the former government forces fled, they destroyed the banks and took all the money with them.

Decapitated Corpses

At a church in Nyamata, two thousand headless corpses lay all huddled together. I was told the people had been rounded up there and that they were then killed with machetés, rifles or hand grenades. Skeletal arms and legs protruded from the corpses' clothes. All the heads had been chopped off with machetés and the skulls were scattered about the church floor. The massacre had taken place only four months before, and the corpses had been left as they were because no relatives were alive to bury them. The nation had its hands too full to do anything about it. Near the corpses were meaningless suitcases, looking as if they had been hurriedly stuffed with belongings. Among the dead bodies were some tiny skulls, on top of which larger bones had been piled—probably mothers killed while trying to protect their babies. I had never seen anything so devastating.

We also visited a Catholic church in Gitarama, on the outskirts of Kigali. Three hundred people had been killed there, having taken refuge in the church in vain. Ten corpses were still there, in a building behind the church. As in the church at Nyamata, the skeletons were still fully dressed.

When my eyes became used to the room's darkness, I noticed a severed head lying at my feet. Its features were still recognizable. Skulls were scattered here and there, including the tiny craniums of small children. I heard that a great many children had been killed. They were too small to run away fast enough. All of them had been beheaded.

It was quiet and still inside the church. Occasionally I could hear the song of a bird. I imagined the cries of death and agony that must have filled the air at the time of the massacre, the angry yells and the screams. The children, exhausted from fleeing, must have heard those cries too.

I am often asked things like, "Weren't you scared standing there?" "Wasn't it spooky?" or "Didn't it smell awful?" I was asked the same questions after I returned from Cambodia. The answer is no. I never felt any of those things. I just felt terribly sorry, and wondered how anyone could have so much hate. That was all I felt.

Mentally Scarred Children

The things that happened in Rwanda were quite different from what happened in the other countries. The murderers were not anonymous guerrillas, but uncles killing their nephews, neighbors, the people next door, the village mayor. People who knew each other well were killing each other.

The survivors knew who the killers were. The killers knew they knew and feared revenge. As a result, everyone was afraid of everyone else.

Someone at the UNICEF office in Kigali told me that just the other day, a girl of twenty-one who worked there suddenly said she would have to quit from the following day. Her parents, brothers and sisters had all been killed. When she was asked why she wanted to leave, she explained, "On my way here just now, I saw the man who killed my family walking toward me. He pretended not to know me, but as he passed he said, right in my ear, 'Oh, I forgot to kill you, didn't I?' So I mustn't stay here a moment longer."

I heard another story. A UNICEF worker said to a little boy in a refugee camp, "Is it true your parents were killed?" The boy replied, "I don't know." The worker imagined he must have been too small to remember and walked away. A little later, the boy came running after the UNICEF worker and said, "I really do know." "Why didn't you say so then?" asked the worker. "Well, you see," the boy said, "the interpreter there with you was the man who killed them." If the boy had let on that he knew—as his family had been murdered before his eyes—there was a danger that he, too, would be killed, for no doubt the interpreter lived in fear of revenge like so many others.

There was an orphanage to the left of the Catholic church where the massacred corpses lay. There were 440 children in the orphanage. It is safe to say that almost all of the surviving children saw their parents and siblings massacred by people they knew well by sight and with whom they had been on good terms right up to the day before the carnage. Every child was living in terror. The older children were filled with hate and carried knives so that if anything happened, they could defend themselves. Every one of them carried a profound pain in his heart as well. Consequently, they were mentally unstable. Some became violent. Some became aphasic and lost their power of speech.

In the refugee camps set up in Rwanda, and neighboring Zaire (the present-day Democratic Republic of Congo), Tanzania, Burundi and Uganda, there were over one hundred thousand children whose parents had either been killed or separated from them. A terrible number. A total of 2.5 million Rwandans—both children and adults—had become refugees.

Whatever orphanage we went to, the teachers would say, "The children don't smile," "You can tell their hearts have been torn apart," "They never cry for their mothers, because they know their mothers will never come back."

Fancy very small children not crying for their moms! The teachers said that if one child started crying in the middle of the night, they would all start crying, and calling out "I'm scared!" or "I don't want to stay here, near those dead people." The teachers said many of the children had developed mental disorders, and it made them heartsick to think of the children growing up like that.

"How it would comfort those children," I thought, "if only a nurse or one of the orphanage teachers could hug them tightly when they woke up in the middle of the night crying, and tell them gently that there was nothing to be frightened of now." What those children needed then, every bit as much as good water, food and medicines, was *love*. But there were not nearly enough people to look after them.

The Smell

We left Kigali and went to the Gikongolo refugee camp. It was one of twenty-eight camps into which the 480,000 people who had been wandering all over the country were now living. On the way, I could see nothing but an expanse of fields. They were fields of coffee, a crop that used to bring in sixty percent of the country's foreign revenue. But it was past harvest time, and nothing had been

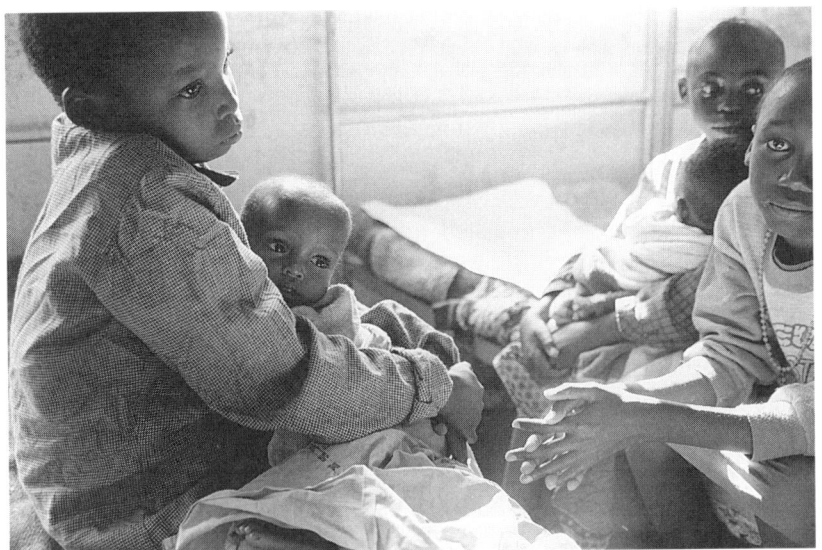

When babies arrive at the orphanage, older children want to mother them. The babies thrive under their care.

done. The harvesters were all either dead or had fled. With nobody to pick the coffee beans they were just rotting on the bushes.

While the TV cameraman was filming the coffee fields, we were aware of a strange smell. At first, we thought it might be the rotting coffee beans. But no, it was the smell of rotting human flesh. Hundreds of corpses had been buried in those very fields.

We smelled it again at the hotel where we stayed that night. We heard that people had been packed into all the hotel rooms like sardines and then slaughtered. The walls had been repapered, but the stench lingered.

There were 680 children in the orphanage at Gikongolo refugee camp. The entrance to the orphanage looked imposing, with an army vehicle full of soldiers posted in front. An institution like that would be an easy target for the enemy, so this was a security precaution. It was hard to understand why anyone would want to kill children who had lost their parents.

In the orphanage courtyard, children were being washed in turn.

There was only a little bit of water in the tub, water being a precious commodity. The children's bellies were distended from malnutrition. There were no bath towels, so after being washed, the children would just sit on a mat until they were dry. It was toward evening, and there was a chilly wind. They all looked cold.

At the orphanage, a girl of seven or eight had a four-week-old baby in her arms. She handled the baby with skill. They were not siblings. Apparently right from the time the orphaned week-old infant was brought there, the older girl eagerly offered to mother her. The teachers at the orphanage said, "When the baby arrived, she was undernourished, and we wondered how to look after her. But she's doing well with the loving care the older girl gives her."

The girl doing the mothering were herself a child at an age when she needed her own mother. She was no doubt reminded of her own lost younger sisters and brothers.

There Are No Devils Left in Hell

It is not easy to try and explain the tragedy of Rwanda simply, for it is a war between ethnic groups, the Hutu and Tutsi. The Hutu were traditionally cultivators who tilled the land and the Tutsi pastoralists who bred cattle. The two lived in relative peace for hundreds of years. Rwanda was a German colony until its administration passed to Belgium at the end of World War I. In the 1920s, the Belgians decided to limit administrative posts and higher education to the Tutsi. Faced with the challenge of deciding exactly who was Tutsi, the Belgians registered all Rwandans as Tutsi or Hutu at the time of their birth. The information was indicated on identity cards which all Rwandans were obliged to carry.

The rift between Hutu and Tutsi deepened in the years before and after independence, especially during the Hutu Revolution in the 1960s. The massacre itself only began after the plane carrying President Habyarimana was shot down on April 6, 1994, the year of my visit. Habyarimana's Hutu supporters blamed the Tutsi and immediately introuced a plan to systematically slaughter them.

Intermarriage between the Hutu and the Tutsi used to be fairly common. A Hutu wife would be told, "We won't kill you, but we're going to kill your Tutsi husband. You've got four children. Half of them have Tutsi blood, so we're going to kill two. Which two shall it be?" I heard that happened many times. Of course a mother couldn't choose. Then they would say, "If you don't choose, we'll kill all four." Hell must be like that.

The massacre triggered an intense civil war. Hutus fearing revenge became refugees and fled to neighboring Zaire. Every day the road to Zaire was clogged with refugees, their number quickly exceeding a million.

But when the Hutus arrived, they found there was no food, no water and no medicine at the refugee camps. Cholera and dysentery broke out as if it were attacking a routed army, killing two thousand people a day, including children. Many of you must have seen the news broadcasts on TV of Rwandans digging deep holes with power shovels and throwing in the bodies to try and prevent infection from spreading. You could see the bodies of small children mingling with larger adult corpses in the enormous shovels. To think that human beings could be born to end like this. I couldn't keep the tears from my eyes.

I remember reading in *Time* magazine the words of a local priest, who said, "There are no devils left in Hell. They are all here in Rwanda."

Boy Soldiers

Thirteen million refugees had fled to Zaire. We went here and there visiting refugee camps. Panzi camp was different from any other I had seen. Many of the boys had been forced to become soldiers. Their ages ranged from eight to sixteen. These children's parents had either been killed or become separated from them.

The boy soldiers wore child-size uniforms and camouflage fatigues. They worked for the eight thousand refugees in Panzi camp who had been soldiers in the former Hutu government forces. They cleaned their rifles, polished their boots, fetched water and cooked their meals. They worked until midnight.

RWANDA, 1994

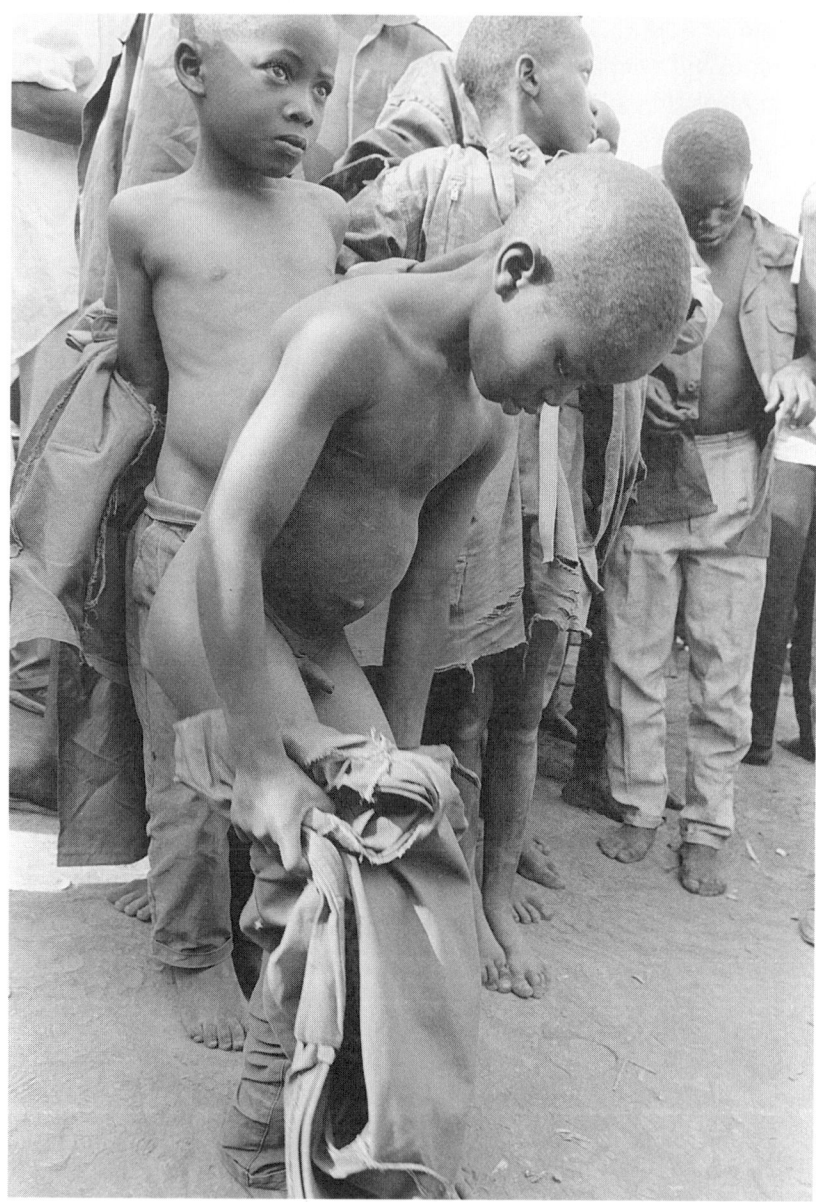

All the boys took off their military uniforms and changed into the children's clothes that we had distributed. Boys as young as these had been made to do the work of soldiers.

UNICEF had succeeded in persuading the soldiers to let the boys take off their uniforms and, instead, wear clothes more suitable for children. UNICEF also arranged for the boys to be moved to a children's camp, where they could study, sing songs and play.

Of the 1,034 children in Panzi refugee camp, 467 had been boy soldiers. An eight-year-old boy who had been a soldier for a month said to me in a tiny voice, "I'm so glad I don't have to be a soldier anymore." When his parents and siblings had all been killed, he had been forced to take up arms. All the children were released from being soldiers.

As I handed out jeans and shirts to the boys, trying to give them clothes that fitted, I said, "Take off what you have on, and don't you ever become soldiers again!"

How the children must have hated those uniforms! When they had taken them off and were standing there stark naked, all of them —even the little ones—threw their uniforms up in the air.

In the United Nations' Convention on the Rights of the Child it stipulates that children must not be used as soldiers. Rwanda had ratified the convention in 1991. But when war breaks out, no one seems to care.

To Love One Another, Hand in Hand

We visited the border town of Goma, where 850,000 of the 1.3 million Rwandan refugees who fled to Zaire were said to be. The figure is overwhelming.

The refugee tents in Goma were pitched right up close to the houses where the people of Zaire lived. Residents said they woke up one morning to find to their immense surprise that several hundred thousand blue vinyl tents had suddenly sprung up all around their homes.

When I met the Zairian governor of the province, he said, "Lots of refugees have come here, but never such an enormous number all at once. They include people working for the former government, the military, politicians—they're all here. It's as if the whole country came. It must be the first time anything like this has happened anywhere in the world. To tell the truth, I think it's an imposition. I think something ought to be done about it."

When I saw the camp, I quite agreed.

Goma refugee camp, in Zaire, was about 215 miles from the capital of Rwanda. Many children had walked all that way alone to escape from the horrors of the massacre. They would finally reach the camp only to die of cholera or to run into the very person who had killed their parents.

From the refugee camp in Goma, you could see the volcano Nyiragongo spewing smoke. Should the volcano have erupted and lava come flowing down, it would have wiped out the camp with its 850,000 refugees. They say the speed of a lava flow can reach forty miles per hour. The tents of the refugees were pitched right on top of an old lava flow.

"So a volcano erupted, did it?" That's all the news would mean to someone living elsewhere. But to the people here who were trying to save as many children's lives as possible, it would be a catastrophe. When I asked them about the volcano, they said, their faces stiffening: "Please don't mention volcanoes. The lava will cover everything. We just try not to think about it."

As for the confrontation between the Hutu and the Tutsi, everyone I met said that Rwanda's future was hopeless. I did meet one person, however, with hope: Dr. Lalani Nimet, a pediatrician who was the head of the orphanage at Ndosho camp in Goma. She was a beautiful lady of about forty, a Belgian of Indian extraction, who had been born and brought up in Zaire. There were two thousand children in the orphanage.

Said Dr. Nimet, "If I didn't believe in peace and hope, why do you think I would be here working like this? Here, these African children should be living in peace. Up to now, they have had nothing but heartbreak. Now is the time to give the children love, to help them to learn and to let them think about what has happened to their country. I want to really get it through to them that when they return to their own country, they mustn't hate one another, but *love one another and build their country, hand in hand.* I firmly believe that's the way to heal Rwanda. I've decided to settle here and see what I can do in the next fifteen years."

An Imposition on the Mountain Gorillas, Too

In Goma's Buhimba camp, there were another two thousand children who had either become separated from their parents or whose parents had been murdered. The children welcomed us by singing and waving their hands. Five hundred of them had some sort of disability and were undergoing treatment and rehabilitation so they could return to society. One of them, a boy of about eight, had a cut on his head that looked as if it had been made with a macheté. His hair had been shaved, making the open wound visible. His parents had been killed, and he had only barely managed to escape. Another boy was on crutches. He had been shot in the leg with a rifle, and the bone was broken. They had operated twice but had not been able to extract the bullet, which was still in his leg. A girl had been shot in the back, and her wound had only just healed. She had a painful-looking scar.

UNICEF was taking pictures of the children to help them find their parents. Children's faces change as they grow, making it difficult for even parents to recognize them. UNICEF was computerizing the relevant data such as the children's names, their parents' names, where they were living, the place where they became separated, and so on.

The person who was taking the photographs said, "The children are so timid and nervous. And they don't smile. You feel they bear a great psychological burden."

To try and make the children laugh, I tried speaking in all sorts of funny ways and singing. They only laughed a little.

Our final visit was to Goma's Kibumba camp. This one, like the others, accommodated about 250,000 refugees. There were so many blue UNHCR tents that they blurred into the distance.

The people had been cutting down trees so rapidly for fuel and heating that an abundant forest nearby had been completely denuded. It had been part of the national park designated by UNESCO as a World Heritage site. The park is the home of the world-famous mountain gorillas. Their habitat is rapidly decreasing because of the refugees going further and further into the forest to seek firewood. It is not surprising that the governor of the province is angry. Many tourists used to come there to see the mountain gorillas. Now, with the refugee camps, hardly any came.

Up to ten people lived in the small tents, each of which was only about six feet by four. They were so close together, there was hardly enough space to walk between them. The refugees were hungry, in a nervous state and always quarreling.

A thin man in his twenties was squatting down cooking some maize gruel over a fire.

The young man indicated that he wanted to say something to me. "What is it?" I asked.

He said, "We haven't had anything to eat except our maize ration, and we don't get much of that. We'd like to have something different sometimes, just for a change."

I asked him when he had last eaten enough to fill his stomach. He said, "Four years ago." He had been on the run for four years during Rwanda's troubles.

"I have no work," he said, "and I don't know what is to become of us. The future seems hopeless. All I can do is just sit and wait for my ration."

I think his words reflected the feelings of everyone in the refugee camp. He was twenty-eight, the age of a working man's prime. It was very sad. But families with a grown man were better off than most. With a baby at her breast and three small children, a young mother whose husband had been killed said that, all alone, she was hard put to even go and fetch water, not to mention their food rations. She showed me her sick baby, who seemed to be dying.

Goma refugee camp, pitched on top of a lava flow, was damp underfoot, now that the rainy season had begun. It was damp in the tents, too. Hygiene was bad, and everyone, both adults and children, was coughing.

The Hutu said it was the Tutsi who had started the fighting; the Tutsi said it was the Hutu. Thus, they continued their endless bloodshed.

It was the adults who were doing the hating. The small children were unaware of what it was all about. Hutu and Tutsi were all the same to them. As I wrote in the Prologue, many children thought it was their fault that their parents and brothers and sisters had been killed. They blamed themselves, thinking their mother had died because they had done something she had told them not to do.

"People were not born to hate one another, they were born to love one another." These words I once heard somewhere had never come into my mind so forcibly as then.

CHAPTER TWELVE

HAITI, 1995

HAITI IS A SMALL COUNTRY SITUATED ON the beautiful Caribbean sea. Columbus encountered the island when he arrived in the Americas. The territory first became a Spanish possession. During this initial period of colonization, the Spaniards killed and drove out the original inhabitants. They then brought over a great many Africans to use as slaves. These Africans are the ancestors of the Haitians. Following the domination of Spain, the western portion of the island was ceded to France. In 1804, Haiti became independent as the first black state in the world.

Unfortunately, ever since its independence it has been under a dictatorship. At its first-ever democratic election, in 1990, President Jean-Bertrand Aristide was elected. Yet only eight months after his inauguration, there was a military coup d'état, and he was forced into exile.

After the coup, a terrible autocratic regime was in power for almost four years. That regime having been overthrown in 1995, President Aristide was able to return from exile in the United States. That was just before my visit. Haiti was now a free country in the real sense. Nevertheless, on account of the long period of political instability, it had become one of the poorest countries in the western hemisphere. Unemployment was eighty percent. How was it possible, I wondered, for eighty percent of a country's population to be out of work? Not surprisingly, slums were taking over the cities.

There was poverty, undernourishment, disease and the breakup of families. The health of the children could not have been worse.

Haiti means "place of many mountains" in the aboriginal language. In accordance with its name, three-quarters of the island is mountainous. However, seen from the air, Haiti's hills and mountains are almost all devoid of trees, cut down for firewood and charcoal. Now, only three percent of the original trees are left. There is no rainy season in Haiti. They have one or two tropical squalls a day. The rain that falls on the denuded hills runs down the slopes and across the plains in torrents until it reaches the lowest places. It makes farming impossible. Thus, farmers have abandoned their villages. The beaches on the Caribbean, which should be beautiful, are brown with mud, an example of how devasting environmental destruction can be.

Haiti's elite, who comprise twenty percent of the population, live high up. Living high up means you have money. Most of the remaining eighty percent, who are poor, live in the low-lying slums. When it rains, the poor are flooded out.

The Street Children Sleep Huddled Together

There are fifteen slums in the capital, Port-au-Prince. We visited one of them, called La Saline, where sixty thousand people live. It had rained the day before. The streets were a quagmire, with puddles of sewage and trash. Children were running around barefoot in it.

The drainage ditches, said to empty into the sea, were clogged up with discarded rubbish, so when it rained, the water had nowhere to go and the slum became flooded. There had just recently been a serious flood in which a lot of people had lost their lives. There were so many people that there was no space in which to install a waste disposal facility.

In the slum, shacks that consisted of a roof and walls of corrugated iron, enclosing about nine feet by six of space, stood cheek by jowl. They reminded me of the shacks put up right after the war in Japan on the ruined sites of the firebombing. Inside, they were like Turkish baths.

HAITI, 1995

Street children have to fend for themselves. At night, perhaps for security, they choose brightly lit places in which to sleep linked together in closely intertwined heaps.

I met a sweet little boy there. His name was Markenson. He was sitting all alone by some trash, looking up at the sky. He said he was twelve, but he was really only about eight or nine. I sat down beside him and said, "Do you come here every day?" He replied, "Yes. I have nothing else to do."

I took his hand and got him to take me to his home.

His home was about eleven feet by six. There were no windows, and it was hot. When my eyes got used to the dark, I could see faces. The only household utensils seemed to be some bamboo baskets. Seven family members lived there.

The grandmother was dandling a crying baby. The baby had a fever and diarrhea. It was obviously suffering from malnutrition and dehydration. The baby's mother was Markenson's sister. She was only fourteen or fifteen. She had curlers in her hair.

There was no sign of either Markenson's father or the baby's father. They had both disappeared. A third of all households in Haiti were single-mother households.

It was around noon. I asked Markenson if they had had anything to eat that day.

"We've had nothing yet today," he replied.

"What about yesterday?"

"We didn't have anything yesterday, either."

"What are you going to do?"

"Mom's out selling water. If she sells enough, she'll buy us something."

My heart ached for these kids. To think that in rich countries there are so many people who complain about eating too much.

In response to my question, "What do you want to do most?" Markenson replied, "I'd like to go to school. I'd like to learn to read and write."

"I'll do my best to make your dream come true," I said.

In Haiti, only twenty-six percent of children go to elementary school.

When I left, I turned to him and said in Japanese, "I have to go now, but try and keep your spirits up."

"Yeah."

"Don't let things get you down."

He would not have understood what I was saying, but I think he knew he had met someone who cared. He looked at me with his great big eyes and nodded. I wished him well with all my heart as I waved good-bye.

It was 8 o'clock at night in Haiti.

The daily temperature of over one hundred degrees had hardly fallen at all.

There was an American music program on the giant TV screen in the outdoor auditorium in Port-au-Prince. Children—big children and little ones—were watching, sprawled on the ground or chatting with their friends. It should have been a happy scene. But those children had no homes, nowhere to sleep and nothing to do. They were street children.

By midnight, all the children were asleep, lying huddled together in storefronts and street squares, holding hands, shoulders touching, some closely overlapping one another. Everyone was connected to someone else as he or she slept.

In the daytime, the street children searched through the trash at street corners or begged. At night, they hung out together. Caring for the street children is a big problem. There are 13,000 such children in institutions. No one knows how many there are wandering the streets.

I met Akiko Sudo, from Japan, who had been engaged in aid activities in Haiti for nineteen years. Miss Sudo was a member of the Christo Roa Missionary Sisters as well as a doctor. She explained to me why there were so many street children.

"Family relations in Haiti are complicated. Most of the people don't look at sexual morals and marriage in the same light that we do. It isn't unusual for a man or a woman to have sex with more than one partner. Many women work to raise children with different fathers. And life is so hard that when children reach the age of about eight, they're turned out of the home and told to go and fend for themselves."

Prostitutes Get Six Gourdes a Turn

Street children kept going in and out of the Central Cemetery. It was the prostitutes' marketplace. The buyers were all men; the sellers were apparently both male and female, mostly children of twelve or thirteen—that is, the equivalent of sixth grade elementary school pupils.

It was known that seventy-two percent of the prostitutes were infected with HIV, the AIDS virus. The figure was fifteen percent for all the people of Haiti, or about one out of every six people. This, too, was a result of poverty.

Nicole, a prostitute at the cemetery, was small and not wearing a dress you would particularly notice. She was only twelve. She had a pocket full of condoms, but she said she didn't make her customers use them if they didn't want to, which happened a lot of the time. "Hey, wouldn't you like to buy me?" she said to our TV Asahi cameraman. When he asked, "How much?" she said, "Six gourdes is OK." That's forty-two yen in Japanese money or about forty cents. These girls were not selling themselves because they wanted to buy brand-name goods. Most did it to feed their families.

To our question, "Aren't you afraid of getting AIDS?" this is what Nicole replied: "I *am* afraid. But even if I get AIDS, I'll live a few years, won't I? You see, my family has no food for tomorrow."

There was nothing we could say.

A couple were embracing on top of a nearby gravestone.

Children were selling their bodies so as not to starve. From them I learned what poverty really meant.

Adding As You Sing

After flying 125 miles north by helicopter, from Port-au-Prince to Anse-Rouge, we visited the Eben Ezer Elementary School there. The school was founded by an NGO and had 234 pupils. It was in a building that looked like a big warehouse. There were no lights, and the five grades were all in one room, with no partitions. Each grade faced a different part of the wall and had its own blackboard.

Pupils were hard at work studying reading, arithmetic and French, the official language. The paint had all worn off the blackboards, leaving just naked wood. You could hardly read what was written on them with white chalk.

What amazed me was when the students were doing addition. First graders were having no trouble at all adding big sums with seven digits! When I listened carefully, I found they were doing it African-fashion, by singing a song: "Six and four is zero, and carry one," they sang in unison.

Alas, only twenty-six percent of children in Haiti enter elementary school. Of those who do, half drop out midway. Moreover, the dropout rate is increasing. This is because the children must look after their brothers and sisters or work in order to help the family finances.

The literacy rate in Haiti is consequently only fifteen percent. Eighty-five percent of the population can neither read nor write. As in so many other countries, illiteracy is due not to laziness but to poverty. The people just have not had a fair chance to study.

No Supplies in the Pediatrics Ward

We visited the State University Hospital back in Port-au-Prince. There were a tremendous number of patients there. In a tent outside the hospital, which was so hot it was like a sauna, the outpatients were being examined.

The pediatrics ward was crowded with babies and children. Six babies, all in one bed, were having intravenous drips. There were many babies suffering from diarrhea and dehydration. As their blood vessels were so small, the drips had to be injected into the veins in their foreheads.

A father proudly showed us a vinyl bag holding the IV fluid that he had bought. At that time in Haiti, one had to buy the intravenous fluid oneself and ask the hospital to administer it. Although there were hospitals, they were short of supplies of every kind.

Further along, the pediatrics ward was filled with children suffering from malnutrition, blood poisoning, typhoid fever and other

HAITI, 1995

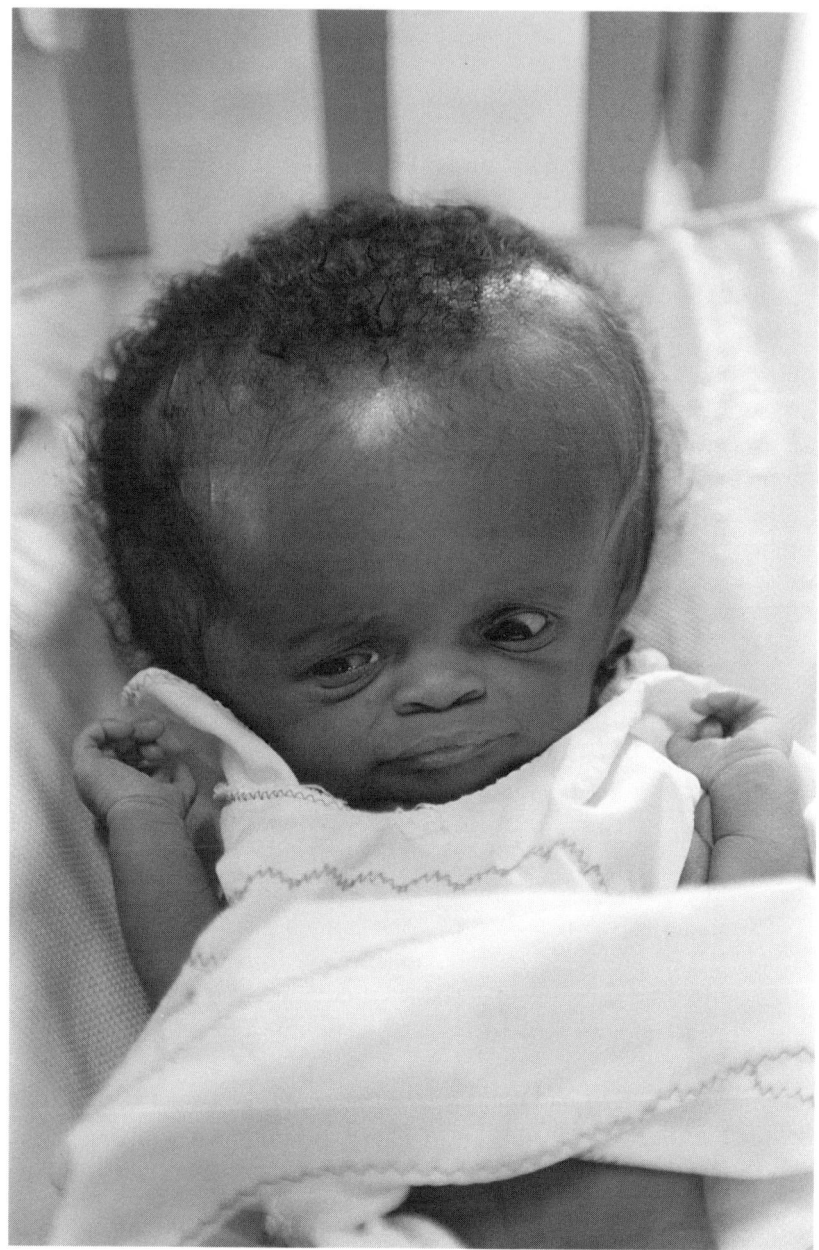

A hydrocephalic baby. Everyone was staring at her, and she looked embarrassed.

ailments. The children with malnutrition were suffering from protein deficiency. Their tummies were so bloated, they looked as if they would burst. They had big purple spots all over their bodies and a few on their faces, too. These children kept their eyes open steadily the whole time because, as the doctor explained, they didn't have the strength to blink. I could understand people not having the strength to open their eyes, but keeping them open without blinking seemed absolutely frightful.

Most of the juvenile patients were abandoned children.

There was a baby there with hydrocephalus (an accumulation of fluid in the brain), who had been abandoned and brought to the hospital. Though her face was normal, her head was swollen to three times the normal size, from the forehead up. Everyone was staring at the child. You could see by her eyes she was embarrassed. The hospital lacked the equipment to draw the fluid out.

In the ward for premature babies, only those expected to survive were in an incubator. Five incubators had been sent from Japan in 1987. The hospital had used them with care, but two of them had broken down, so only three were left. The doctor said he wished they knew how to fix them.

The other premature infants who weren't able to be in an incubator were laid out in a row, like objects, on a sort of small table. They were all thin, with puny little arms and legs, and their cheekbones and ribs showing. It was quite pathetic to see. The expressions on their faces were all so terribly sad. Now and again, a nurse would come and give them a shake, to see if they were still alive. The nurses weren't exactly rough with them, it was just that there were not enough helpers to go around, and they were busy.

"We'd like to save them," said the doctor and the nurses, "but there is nothing we can do. We just haven't the resources."

While I was watching, one of the preemies raised both its little arms. As I wondered what had made it to do that, its arms suddenly stopped in midair. A nurse who was nearby pressed her stethoscope firmly against its chest and said the child had died.

The baby seemed as if it had just taken a deep breath and dropped one of its arms. The other arm remained fixed in the air. Its eyes were closed, as if it had given up the struggle.

HAITI, 1995

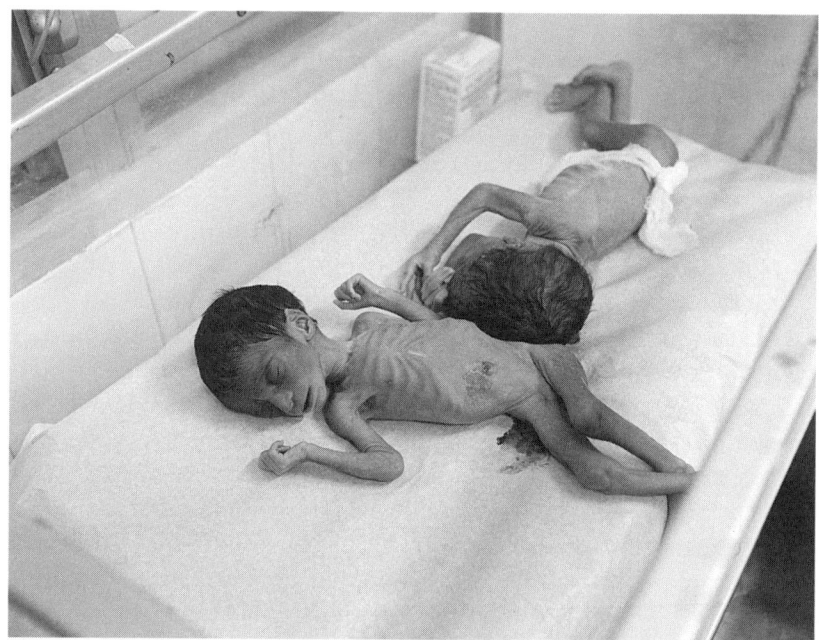

Babies who could not be put in incubators, because there were not enough to go around. Born in vain!

There was a child in the next room with a white cloth over his face. He was about one year old, with spindly legs less than an inch thick. It was the first time I had seen a dying child—not in a refugee camp or on a roadside—brought to a state university hospital, where nothing at all could be done for him. It was pitiful. And his parents were nowhere to be seen. If the child had to die, how much happier at least to die in someone's arms. He had been brought to a hospital, only to die there all alone. I had to grit my teeth to keep myself from crying.

Babies with Aids

In Port-au-Prince, there was a hospice for children run by an American Christian organization.

There was a small baby there with AIDS. It was a boy, six months old, whose mother had given birth to him just before she died, after having suffered from AIDS for seven years.

The baby had an adult's eyes. He seemed to be looking far off into the distance. I said to him, "You didn't want to be sick, did you? You should have been born healthy. What bad luck to be born with something like this. But you must get better!" His faraway eyes then turned to me. He seemed to have understood what I said.

Suddenly, the baby took his hands from his chest, where they had been, and brought them to his mouth, as if he wanted to say something. He hadn't learned to talk, and yet he desperately wanted to tell me something. I put my face close to his and said, "Yes, I know. I do understand." The child moved his tiny lips as if he wanted to tell me his troubles. I listened for some time to his silent appeal. That was the only thing I could do for that baby dying of AIDS. It was a trying time for me.

It became time for us to go. When I said good-bye, the child's eyes moved off in a flash to that faraway place. His expression became one of resignation.

I would have liked to stay there with him for a long time listening to him because, while he was talking to me, his eyes looked like a living baby's eyes.

I tried to talk to another child, a girl who had also been infected with AIDS, but there was no response whatsoever.

A paper mobile, suspended from the ceiling, kept turning around and around.

This hospice was the only one of its kind in Haiti. The children were lucky to be there, surrounded by kind doctors and nurses.

Most of the children in Haiti just died somewhere or other, all alone, without being hugged by anyone or having someone around to whom they could tell what they felt.

Granny's Breast

UNICEF, together with the World Health Organization (WHO), was promoting breast-feeding. A campaign was underway in Haiti.

Because economic sanctions had been in force against Haiti for a long time, powdered milk was too expensive for poor people to buy. Mothers were feeding their children flour mixed with unsafe water, or just warm water with sugar in it. This meant that a great many children suffered from malnutrition. Mother's milk, on the other hand, was safe, hygienic, cost nothing and helped to protect babies from disease.

I was invited to an award ceremony, in the northwestern town of Gros-Morne, for fifty mothers who had fed their babies for six months on nothing but breast milk. They were going to be given commendation certificates.

I saw something at this ceremony that astonished me. A white-haired grandmother was breast-feeding an infant. She seemed to be producing milk with tremendous vigor. The baby was her grandchild. It was fifteen years since the woman had last given birth, and yet she had successfully breast-fed her grandchild.

The television station staff that accompanied me refused to believe it. "It's weird," they cried. But nobody in that village thought it surprising at all. In Haiti, they have a saying, "If Mother has no milk, get it from Granny." Isn't that marvelous! They also say, "Love the child and your milk will flow."

We visited a prison for women and children. There were 70 women prisoners and 101 children. Cruel treatment at the hands of their husbands had driven most of the women to crime.

In the prison workshop the women were learning dressmaking to provide them with the skills needed for them to get a job as soon as they were released. The children were learning how to repair electric wiring. They were cheerful and said things like, "When I get out I want to do this kind of work." With eighty percent unemployment, however, there was no work to be had. The adults in the institution were worried about the children.

Most of the kids were street children. Some had been picked up just for sleeping on the streets. Some of the small ones had been caught acting as lookouts for prowlers, all of whom got away.

Prisoners are usually jailed for crimes such as theft, murder and drug addiction. The women and children I met had no idea what their crimes were, nor how long a sentence they had been given. They were just in prison, that was all. There had been no trial, no lawyers, no proper judgment.

I told President Aristide about my visit and said, "If people are to be put in prison, please let them be judged by the law first. Otherwise, children will grow up not to trust adults."

A Hotline to the President

"The Family Is Life" institution for street children was started by President Aristide. The dilapidated building was undergoing repairs. It had been attacked twice during the time of the military dictatorship, on account of its connection with Aristide. Many children had been killed. When I went there, it accommodated seventy street children between the ages of eight and sixteen.

The first thing the children did was perform two pieces of music for me, "The Land of Sunshine," which was about Haiti, and a piece called "Forgetting." They called their band Intravenous Injection. The group was made up entirely of boys, with drums, keyboard, guitars and bongos. They played us lots of music with typical Caribbean melodies and rhythms. The band leader and vocalist was an eleven-year-old orphan with a resolute face.

They asked us to sing something in Japanese. Without hesitation, I obliged by singing "Sukiyaki." All the children in the room were completely captivated and started singing along with me. They clapped their hands, adding some instruments and moving their bodies to the rhythm. We sang on and on.

"Look, these Haitian children are singing your song!" I said in my heart as I looked up toward heaven, where I was sure Hachidai Nakamura was.

When I said it was time for us to go, the children played "Auld Lang Syne" for us as we left.

There would be no work for them when they went out into society, but the children were not discouraged. They held on to their dreams and tried as hard as they could to live in a forward-looking way.

Two days later, I met President Aristide. He said there was a direct telephone line between The Family Is Life and the president, and that he had told the children they could telephone him anytime they wanted, if they had something they wished to say.

The President told me the band leader had rung him up at midnight on his telephone, which was in his bedroom, to report that the UNICEF goodwill ambassador had been there and to say how thrilled they all were. The boy mentioned that she had taught them a Japanese song, which they all sang together. When she left, she was crying, the boy said. They were so happy that someone felt warmly enough about them to shed tears for them. "And please tell her how grateful we all were."

Yes, there were tears in my eyes when they played "Auld Lang Syne." Fancy their noticing them and telephoning the president! The sensitivity of those boys amazed me. I saw how important people's love and even people's tears must be to children.

Finally, President Aristide said to me, "The most important thing is education. That's the only thing that can save this country. In the next three years, I'd like to raise the literacy rate from fifteen to eighty-five percent. When we have achieved this, Miss Kuroyanagi, please come and visit us again."

I promised I would.

Right now, in Japan, I hear that Jamaica is a fashionable honeymoon location. Haiti is very near Jamaica. I hope Haiti will soon become a country where couples will want to spend their honeymoon. It may well be that the future of this beautiful country on the Caribbean Sea depends on its literacy rate rising to eighty-five percent.

CHAPTER THIRTEEN

BOSNIA-HERZEGOVINA, 1996

I HAD BEEN ASKING TO GO TO BOSNIA-HERZEGOVINA for the last few years, but it was considered too dangerous. On a trip I took to Yugoslavia as a young girl, I thought Dubrovnik was the most beautiful town that ever was. I heard it had been bombed. It was terribly sad to think of people wailing and crying there, while just next door, in Italy, tourists were shopping without a care in the world and, in neighboring Austria, they were happily listening to Viennese waltzes.

The dispute that began in 1991 in what was formerly Yugoslavia was perhaps the worst thing to happen in Europe since World War II. Many regions became battlefields, cities and farming communities were attacked, and people's lives were ruined.

Yugoslavia had been a federation of six republics. For many years, it had functioned as a single nation. In 1991, three of the republics—Slovenia, Croatia and Macedonia—seceded and became independent.

In 1992, civil war broke out in Bosnia-Herzegovina when the republic declared its independence.

The war started out as a confrontation between the anti-independence Serbs and the pro-independence Muslims and Croats. As their leaders stirred up hatred and fear of each other, fighting intensified.

The dispute between the peoples of the former Yugoslavia is

extremely complicated. They say that even among experts there are only a few who really understand it. Only one thing is certain: it has been very hard indeed on the women and children.

The crux of the war has been something called "ethnic cleansing," in which the basic idea is to kill off everyone of another race, in order to leave only people of one race in the country. Women and children were especially targeted. Part of the strategy was to murder the children of the other race and rape the women so that any children they bore would be of one's own race.

The population of Bosnia-Herzegovina was 3.5 million in 1994. In three and a half years of war, 150,000 were killed or missing. More than 2.5 million people were driven from their homes and had fled to other countries as refugees or were displaced within their own country.

It was about 125 miles, as the crow flies, from Belgrade, the capital of the former Yugoslavia, to Sarajevo, in Bosnia. About 220 miles separated Belgrade from Zagreb, in Croatia.

Originally, in Bosnia-Herzegovina, the Muslims (forty-four percent of the population), the Serbs (thirty-one percent) and the Croats (seventeen percent) had all been living fairly amicably together.

What, Me? Arrested on Suspicion of Being a Spy?

Six months after the conclusion of the Dayton peace accord, we set off in a bus from Zagreb, the capital of the Republic of Croatia, for Mostar, a town in the south of Bosnia-Herzegovina. It was a long, thirteen-hour journey.

There was yellow tape stretched all along both sides of the road. It had the words "Halt! Land Mines" printed on it. Beyond the tape, there were mainly fields full of beautiful flowers. Those fields were also littered with land mines, and one was told not to set foot there under any circumstances.

Ten million land mines lay buried in what was the former Yugoslavia, three million of those in Bosnia-Herzegovina alone. According to a land mine distribution map, most of Bosnia-Herzegovina was a danger zone.

Land mines cost no more than three dollars each. To remove them costs from three hundred to a thousand dollars. How on earth were they going to remove such a quantity?

Wherever you looked, there was nothing but green meadows. It was hard to believe there were land mines out there. The dwellings dotted here and there had orange roofs and white walls. It was a dreamlike landscape. However, when you looked closer, you could see that many of the roofs had been blown away, and the stone walls were badly crumbled.

GOODWILL AMBASSADOR KUROYANAGI ARRESTED ON SUSPICION OF BEING A SPY, said a Japanese newspaper headline. The incident happened on the way to Mostar, in a little town in the west of Bosnia called Drvar.

As we drove toward the town, halfway up a hill we saw the name TITO made out of tree branches. President Tito had led the resistance to Hitler when the Germans invaded Yugoslavia during World War II. It was he who liberated the country. Tito is still greatly revered in what was formerly Yugoslavia. In Dvar, a place connected with the resistance movement, there was a cave in which President Tito was said to have hidden.

We had stopped the bus and were looking at the cave, which was a hundred yards further on, when suddenly we were told to come to the police station nearby. They said we had photographed a policeman's face, though in fact we hadn't photographed anything.

The monstrous thing was that the police were actually after the brand new eighteen-seater rental bus we had come in. Intending to steal it, they first picked a quarrel.

Our Muslim driver was taken inside the police station. We found out later that the police chief had said to him things like, "It's you people who killed us Croatians," and "You killed my parents and my brothers and sisters." For three hours they hurled such accusations at him. If our Muslim driver had retaliated, saying "And what about you Croatians?" the police chief would probably have shot him dead with his pistol. The driver simply kept on apologizing for those three hours, thus saving his life. We were inside the bus and knew nothing of what was happening.

There was hardly any traffic on the road.

While we waited, I went to the only shop that was open and bought some tomatoes and cheese. We were given some bread by a policeman going home. I had recently played the part of a ninety-two-year-old lady in a drama at the Ginza Saison Theater in Tokyo, so I made the people in the bus laugh by reciting lines from the play in my old-lady voice, such as "What can you possibly want by arresting an old lady like me, with only a few years left?"

After detaining us for over three hours, they confiscated the bus. We were put on board an old minibus provided by the police, who impounded two of our empty videotapes, several rolls of film and five hundred marks in payment for their minibus, before they released us.

We heard afterwards from an authority that not having shown any fear worked in our favor. If we had looked scared, the police probably would have taken advantage by stealing our money, cameras and other things, perhaps killing us into the bargain, while the outside world remained uninformed of the event, and we were reported as merely missing.

Even though they say that peace in the region is guaranteed now, this incident taught me that the reality is different. It also made clear to me the seriousness of the ethnic problems that now exist in what was once Yugoslavia.

Later, in Sarajevo, UNICEF reported the incident to Interpol, who demanded an apology from the foreign minister and the minister of state in Croatia. This news appeared in the papers of many countries, including Japan, which is how the story originated that I'd been arrested as a spy.

Children's Radio

The city of Mostar, in the south of Bosnia-Herzegovina, takes its name from the Slavic word *most*, meaning "bridge." It is an ancient city which flourished for five hundred years under the rule of the Ottoman Empire. Most of its inhabitants are Muslims, the followers of Islam.

The Neretva River which flows through the center of the city is the color of turquoise. The beautiful stone bridge that crossed it was particularly famous. That bridge, built by the Turks 430 years ago and a precious part of the world's heritage, is now only to be seen on picture postcards. It lies in ruins, having been destroyed by shells. Its place has been taken by a swaying suspension bridge. The beautiful rows of houses, too, remain only on postcards. The Croatians, with their bombardments, reduced the town to rubble.

The population of Mostar was 102,000. Out of that, 45,000 had become refugees, 5,000 were wounded and 2,000 were killed. All buildings worthy of the name were damaged beyond repair.

Before the civil war began, Croatians, Serbians and Muslims intermingled and lived together in relative harmony. Then Croatians and Muslims started attacking each other according to which side of a particular road in Mostar they lived on. This road, which separated east from west, was about eight or nine yards wide. They were people who, up until the day before, had been neighbors and friends. An international peacekeeping force removed the land mines, but it was not until March 1996, that traffic was finally able to use the road again.

The buildings in Mostar were roofless, and their white walls were pitted with trench-mortar holes. I counted over three hundred holes in one wall. I wondered why they had to fire so many shells. I had the same thought about a school bus, abandoned on the road, that was riddled with bullet holes. Wherever you looked, the ruins spoke of nothing but hate.

Even at the peak of the civil war in Bosnia-Herzegovina, devoted teachers held classes in safe places, such as basements. In addition to their ordinary lessons, children learned how to escape death from dangers such as land mines.

We visited Zelik Elementary School. Before the war, it had been a school with some extremely modern courses on its curriculum. They even used computers. But now it was short of notebooks and pencils.

The headmistress was a Ms. Rizuanovic. She said most of the children had had terrible experiences and had seen people being killed in the fighting. Because of this, some had become emotionally unstable and had shut themselves off from the outside world, being unable

BOSNIA-HERZEGOVINA, 1996

Although there were hundreds of shell holes in the white wall of their house, this family was fortunate to be able to live there together.

to speak and unable to sleep at night. Some little girls I had spoken to by the small school gate certainly were quite unsmiling.

The headmistress herself was a refugee. She went on, in a low voice, "My husband, who was an economist, was killed by the Croatian forces. I had two sons, aged seventeen and twenty-two. They were at a school some distance from where we lived and were drafted into the Croatian army. The younger boy was killed. The older one was captured by radicals and taken to a camp. It was like a Nazi concentration camp. He was beaten and, I believe, badly hurt. I still haven't seen him. But I haven't had as bad a time as many other people, although we've all been through more or less the same experiences."

And to think they were all citizens of the same country such a short time ago! How such a tragic situation could come about is hard for those of us who live in stable societies to imagine.

That evening, after we arrived in the Bosnian capital of Sarajevo, I took part in a local radio program. It was a program put on entirely by children and was quite famous. The program, supported by UNICEF, provided a lot of ideas on the kind of education and entertainment that would help to rehabilitate the minds of children affected by the war.

The announcers and interviewers were all children. Thirteen-year-old Asja Jevtic was an extremely popular disc jockey. She wanted me to give a message to the children of Sarajevo. I said I hoped they would never let go of their dreams, whatever the circumstances. I sang a verse from "Sukiyaki." Its message is that no matter how unhappy you are, if you keep your head up to keep your tears from falling, happiness will surely come.

Ethnic Cleansing

It is well known that on June 28, 1914, in Sarajevo, Archduke Ferdinand, the crown prince of Austria, and his consort, were assassinated by a young Serb, thereby triggering World War I.

The city hall from which the archduke and archduchess set out that day became a national library after World War II. The structure, built two hundred years earlier, was until then famous as a library housing a large collection of valuable medieval documents. I heard that this library had been badly damaged.

I stood amid the ruins of the national library for a long time. The extent of its destruction was unimaginable. I wondered how it was possible to destroy a stone building so completely. Everything connected with the heritage of mankind in Europe during the Middle Ages was lost or destroyed.

All that was left was an interesting architectural feature on the second floor gallery that used perspective to make something close look as if it were far off.

The large *Oslobdjenje* newspaper building had collapsed entirely in the bombing, except for the parts at each side where the elevators were. The ruins presented a fearful sight. The pretty painted walls of a home for the elderly were riddled with bullet holes. The roof had been blown away, together with the dreams of the elderly people who had happily lived there. Here and there, the road had substantial shell holes that had become puddles of water.

Some of you may remember hearing in the news of the large bomb thrown into an open-air market in Sarajevo, in the winter of 1994, on a day when it was crowded with shoppers, sixty of whom died at one stroke.

The Winter Olympics were held in Sarajevo in 1984. The roof and seats of the indoor skating rink, next to the place where the opening ceremony was held, were so badly destroyed in the bombing that it looked as if an avalanche had crushed them. Right under the Olympic mascot character painted on the wall were several bullet holes. The whole of the soccer stadium had been turned into a cemetery. A look at the gravestones showed that most of the people buried there had lost their lives in the internecine warfare between 1992 and 1995.

An elderly woman, who appeared to be in her eighties, was cleaning one of the graves, her eyes red with tears.

"He was my only son," she said. "He was a technician, and only forty. He was killed in a Serbian bombing raid. My daughter-in-law and grandchildren moved to an area controlled by the Serbs, so I can't see them."

You could tell by the name on the gravestone that she and her family were Serbs. Her Serbian son had been killed by Serbs, just because he was in Sarajevo. That was the kind of war it was.

The old lady told us all this with tears in her eyes. Then, stroking my cheeks with her hands, she said, "I have no one left. I have no one left. I am all alone."

Dobrinja, where the Olympic village had been, was one of Sarajevo's biggest new towns. Its population had once been forty-five thousand, but so many had been killed or become refugees that there were only twenty thousand people left.

There was a bridge about forty feet long in the middle of the new town that had sandbags piled up high on either side. Its span was lined with wrecked cars, which served as a shield for people crossing the bridge to protect them from sniper shots. It was known as "sniper's alley."

I tried running across the bridge in a crouching position. The snipers' fire came from half a mile away. At the sound of the first round of fire, you hide behind a sandbag and then run across the bridge in the brief interval between that and the next flurry! Even if you were more than a quarter of a mile away, your face could be seen closeup in the snipers' telescopic sights. It was scary. It didn't matter whether you were a child or a woman: the snipers were ordered to fire at anything that moved.

According to UNICEF's 1993 survey, ninety-seven percent of the children in Sarajevo had personally experienced a shell attack, twenty-nine percent frequently experience unbearable sadness, and twenty percent had terrible nightmares regularly. About fifty-five percent of the children had been shot at by snipers, and sixty-six percent had found themselves in circumstances where they thought they were going to die. Experiences such as these leave deep scars on a child's psyche, resulting in nightmares, panic attacks, anxiety and many other problems. What dreadful statistics these are.

I'd Like to Be Zero Years Old

In Dobrinja, the one-time Olympic Village, we visited a preschool drawing class. It was a UNICEF-supported project for healing children's psychological scars.

The classroom was in semidarkness, since the windows had been cemented over and sandbags were piled up outside. It was an air-raid shelter that had served to protect the children from attack and had been left just as it was. And that was six months after the Dayton peace accord had been signed!

It made me feel nervous. Did they think something might start happening again?

The children were making things and drawing pictures. This expressive activity was supposed to help them bring disturbing thoughts to the surface and relive horrific memories. There were no smiling faces among the children.

I extemporized a puppet play with some stuffed toys, which made the children laugh a little.

I thought of the pictures drawn by children that I had seen at the library in Zagreb. The theme was "What I Want to Be Most of All." And what did they want to be? Almost all of the children drew pictures of babies. I suppose the poor darlings thought if they could become babies again, they would escape the horrors of the war.

A nine-year-old boy had drawn a very intense picture of a figure that looked like a black robot, with a large zero in its middle. "I'd like to be zero years old," he wrote underneath it. "Then I'd be inside my mom's tummy."

A nine-year-old girl had painted a blue picture of herself and then covered it over with black paint. She wrote, "I want to become twenty-five right away and be a Hollywood star." It was a wild dream, but I suppose she was just trying to escape from her present self.

There was also a picture of a tank painted in dark blue and black, and another that looked like dynamite done in black and reddish brown. The first bore the message, "A tank for my beloved Denis," and the other, "This bomb is a present for Irena." Not the sort of thing you would ever see in a country at peace.

The explanation under a picture of the artist's face reflected in a mirror, and painted with red and green lines was, "My face was blown off by a bomb, and this is what I look like." But the child who wrote that had not, in fact, been injured.

The psychiatrist in charge told me that most of the children who were deeply disturbed painted with two colors. The deeper their mental scars, the further they wanted to get away from themselves. This they often did by pretending to be somebody else.

After we left Zagreb, we passed woods filled with white acacias, all in bloom. It was such a peaceful scene, it was hard to believe that a civil war had been going on for four years.

Yet the children were indeed mentally disturbed and suffering from their memories of the horror.

Only Black Paint

At an orphanage in Zenica, near Sarajevo, there were sixty-five orphans being cared for, from the age of six months up to eighteen

BOSNIA-HERZEGOVINA, 1996

A boy at the orphanage was getting black paint on his desk as well as his picture. Will his deep mental scars ever be healed?

years old. The parents of some of them had been killed in the war. Others had become separated from their families while they were fleeing as refugees.

UNICEF was helping to find some of the parents. They said fifteen children had so far been reunited with their parents.

In the room where they were working to alleviate the mental distress of the children, a number of them were painting pictures. The under-fours belonged to a generation that had known nothing but war. The pictures they painted were only of war.

Among them was a boy who was painting away for all he was worth on a sheet of orange-colored drawing paper. The paint he was using was black. He was painting so vigorously that his strokes were going off the paper and onto the desk. He had got black paint on his face, too. I said to him, "Dear me, that won't do, will it, getting paint on your desk like that."

He managed a shy titter, although the teachers said the children hardly ever smiled.

"Why not try using some red? It would look pretty," I said. Whereupon he replied at once, "I don't like red. I like black," and continued slapping on the black paint.

The boy was eight or nine. When I said, "How old are you?" he replied, "I don't know." Apparently, he didn't remember anything. There were lots of children like that.

Perhaps when too many horrors and terrible experiences keep on happening, God kindly provides amnesia to wipe them out of the mind. But then that too is a kind of horror.

A Stuffed Animal Bomb

The elementary and middle schools that were destroyed during the four-year war in ex-Yugoslavia had been left just as they were. Those schools that were lucky and had escaped destruction were being used as camps for refugees and the homeless.

Only a very few classrooms were kept for schoolwork, and these were jam-packed. With so many pupils, there were not enough teachers, school furniture, textbooks and other necessities to go around. Lipik Elementary School, in the Republic of Croatia, was one such school.

Classes had to accommodate middle- as well as elementary-grade pupils. The corridor walls were covered with "Beware of Land Mines" posters. In classes, pupils were shown photographs and videos of various types of land mines, as well as examples of the real thing, stressing their danger over and over. It made me miserable to think that instruction regarding land mines and weapons had to be given such precedence, when there were so many other things they should have been studying.

To the teacher's question, "Have any of you found a land mine yourself?" practically every hand went up. The pupils described the experience variously: "I found one in the forest," "I found one in my uncle's corn field," "I found one near our house," or "We were playing soccer, and when I went to pick up the ball, it was near a land mine."

As mentioned earlier, as many as ten million land mines had been buried in what was once Yugoslavia.

The slightest touch will cause a mine to explode. Adults lose arms and legs. With treatment, however, they survive. But children are small and weak, and usually die. If they are lucky enough to survive, they lose arms and legs and sustain serious injuries to their intestines and reproductive organs. A great many children have lost their eyesight simply from the blast of a land mine.

I never would have thought there could be mines and bombs specifically targeting children. I found it hard to believe that anyone could do that.

There were plastic booby traps scattered about on the ground shaped like ice-cream cones. Small children would pick them up, thinking that's what they were. Just as a child started to eat the cone, it would go off, killing it.

I heard there were even booby traps shaped like chocolate Easter eggs wrapped in silver paper. The bombs would go off when the silver paper was unwrapped. There were bombs shaped like toy motorcars, too.

As I wrote in the Prologue, bombs were even hidden inside stuffed animals. As the fighting became worse, families were forced to flee from their homes. Perhaps a child would want to take a teddy bear too, but Mom would probably say no, you'll have to leave it behind, as she took her child by the hand and they ran for their lives. When the attack was over, they would go back to their house, and there was the beloved teddy bear! But it would explode as the happy child picked it up. While the house was empty, someone had put a bomb inside the toy.

Little bells would fall from the sky. The bells exploded when they hit the ground. Lots of them, though, got caught in the trees. Children would see the strings hanging down from the trees and be intrigued. When they pulled on the strings the bells would fall to the ground and explode.

All children love things that look like fun, and they were hungry, too. Fancy studying child psychology in order to kill children! The perpetrators must have had children of their own, as well. War makes people think up such devilish things.

A Father's Tears

At a refugee camp in Macedonia, one of the republics of the former Yugoslavia, I was given a letter from a mother and her children—a thirteen-year-old son and ten-year-old daughter—to be delivered to their father. The three of them had fled to Macedonia from Gorazde, in Bosnia-Herzegovina. They had had no news of the father for four years. Now that the war was over and a peace accord had been signed (in December 1995), their father, if he was alive and well, would probably have gone back to their home. They wanted to let him know that they were safe. They said letters sent by refugees rarely reached their destination.

We went to Gorazde and managed to find the father's house. He had indeed returned there. The buildings of Gorazde, which is surrounded by low hills, had been the targets of attack. The walls were riddled with bomb and bullet holes. There had been severe fighting there right up to the end.

I handed the father the letter from his wife, son and daughter. There was a look of incredulity on the small man's face as he slit open the envelope. "Yes, it's my wife's writing, all right," he said as he began to read the letter. It contained snapshots as well. He stared at them avidly.

We had also brought him a tremendous surprise: a video we had taken of his family!

"I'd have recognized my son," he said as he watched it, "but my daughter has grown so much I never would have recognized her. How thin she is. When I last saw her she was plump. I see my wife still has her dimples!"

We left him to watch the video alone. Peeking, I noticed that although he was smiling, there were tears rolling down his cheeks.

Afterwards, he told us how when the war started, they found themselves surrounded by the enemy. All he could think of was helping his wife and children escape. He then had to become a soldier and fight. His intention had been to go and fetch them as soon as possible, but the war dragged on for years. He had had no news of his family. The chemical plant where he had worked had been destroyed, and he was out of work and had no money. Although freedom of movement was guaranteed in principle, there were more and more incidents where people had been attacked. He had been nervous of trying to get to the refugee camp. He didn't know for sure whether his wife and children were alive.

As we parted, he said, "What on earth do you think I ought to do now?"

The war had separated so many families in this way.

At a home for the aged in Petrinja, the elderly were cared for regardless of which side they were on. They were old men and women who had been left behind when the war started.

There was an old man of eighty who seemed to have lost his will to live.

"My son is dead," he said, "and so is my wife. My daughter-in-law is a Serb, and I don't know where she went. I wish they would find her. No, it's my grandchild I want to see."

It was the same at the refugee camps and shelters for the homeless. The men had lost hope and said little.

It was the women who were strong and optimistic. A woman of about seventy said, happily, "It's nice here. There are no bullets flying about. Everyone is kind, and we're getting along fine."

In Africa and the other countries I have been to, the women have been the cheerful ones, rather than the men. When men lose whatever it is they have established and built up, they seem to be struck down. I suppose they tend to cling to their ideals, whereas women are more realistic.

That even applied to an old homeless woman living in a shelter at the back of an elementary school in Gorazde. She was seventy-eight. One eye was partly cloudy and she couldn't see well with the other. She only had one tooth left, and no shoes. Her husband had died. Of her three sons, one had been killed in the war, one had been badly injured and was in Sarajevo, and she didn't know what had happened to the third.

She had no belongings. As she smiled and showed me her one remaining tooth, she said, "I was still a girl at the time of World War II, and I could speak lots of languages. Of course I spoke English. My English was good, yes, good."

"How wonderful!" I said.

"Yes," she went on, "everything was good. And now, it is good just to be alive. That is good, good, good!"

I looked at the lady's bare feet. Her heels were full of cracks.

We Were Born to Love One Another

It was at the time the civil war in Bosnia-Herzegovina had become worse than ever. There was a popular cafe in the main square in the town of Tuzla. The twenty-fifth of May was a holiday called Young People's Day. Even though it was in the middle of a civil war, there were young people gathered there. Suddenly, a bomb came flying over and exploded. Seventy-one people were killed, aged between three and seventeen. More than two hundred were injured.

When we visited the town a year later, in 1996, the square was piled high with flowers, and the flames of countless candles were flickering in the breeze.

I asked a young girl who she was lighting a candle for. "A classmate," she replied, and continued, "I just can't talk about it." She remained silent, praying for her friend.

Nearby, on a wall, were photographs of the young victims. There were children among them. People were gathered together in front of the photographs.

A middle-aged woman, mopping her eyes with a handkerchief, said her niece had died there. I looked at her picture. She was a very pretty girl. There was also a picture of a handsome young man to whom she had been engaged. They had both been killed.

It is easy to say, well, there was a war on. But just imagine seventy-one young people in your own neighborhood killed in the twinkling of an eye by a single flying bomb—people who had been laughing and talking together up until that moment. Then imagine the grief of their families.

As we walked about, people on crutches, minus legs, were much in evidence.

You could see that the terror of a war in which you never knew when you might be the next victim had been deeply etched into the minds of many of the young. I heard that a good number were given to crying fits, attempting suicide, becoming severely depressed, or having bouts of aggression that led to crime.

Before the civil war, Muslims, Serbs and Croats lived together peacefully in Bosnia-Herzegovina. If they were able to do so, why did they have to start hating and killing each other just for being of a different race? Why the killing of children or the raping of elementary school pupils as part of their strategy?

The children I saw in orphanages, elementary schools, refugee camps and shelters seemed cheerful enough on first acquaintance. And these children, unlike those in the African countries I had visited, were not thin and emaciated. But many had deep psychological scars from the horrors of war and sexual violence. All were in need of psychiatric treatment.

There were also a great many children from destitute or refugee families, who had either not been able to go to school or had been absent from school for a long time. When I was there, one could not say that peace had been wholly established.

BOSNIA-HERZEGOVINA, 1996

Did you notice in the opening parade at the Atlanta Olympic Games how five placards had taken the place of the single one that used to be YUGOSLAVIA? This time there were athletes carrying placards that said SLOVENIA, CROATIA, MACEDONIA and BOSNIA-HERZEGOVINA. The fifth said NEW YUGOSLAVIA, a federation of Serbia and Montenegro.

The athletes entered the arena smiling happily. But a lot of blood had been shed in their various countries. Children were still frightened of land mines. They were having nightmares about them and had lost their faith in people.

We were not born to hate one another, we were born to love one another.

I am sure anyone would agree. What concerns the people of that region concerns us all.

EPILOGUE

All the children I met
Were beautiful.
Laughing children, mischievous children,
Little girls with babies on their backs,
Boys showing off their somersaults,
Children I sang songs with,
Children who followed me everywhere.
I met all sorts of children.
And children, too, whose parents
And brothers and sisters
Had been slaughtered right before their eyes.
Children with arms and legs cut off by guerrillas,
Girls whose parents had disappeared,
Leaving them with baby brothers and sisters to look after.
Boys forlorn because their friends,
The domestic animals, had starved to death.
Children whose homes and schools had been destroyed.
Orphans, shunted from one camp to another.
Children who worked as prostitutes to support their families.

And yet,
Even in terrible circumstances such as these,
They told me not one child had committed suicide.
Not one, in any of the refugee camps,
Although they had no future and no hope.
I asked about it, everywhere I went.
"Haven't any children killed themselves?"
"No, not a single one."
And I wept.

EPILOGUE

As I watched emaciated children,
Virtual skeletons, hurrying by
With all their might and main,
I wept.
I wanted to shout out loud,
"In Japan, children kill themselves!"
Is there anything sadder?
What does affluence mean? What is abundance?

After meeting all these various children,
I want to say this to the children of Japan:
If you feel sorry for children in developing countries,
Whom you have met in this book,
And want to help them,
Say right now to your friend
Sitting next to you,
"Let's get along with each other.
Let's join hands and go through life together."
At my elementary school—Totto-chan's school—
There were several handicapped children.
My best friend
Was a boy with polio.
The headmaster never once said,
"Be kind to those children," or "Help them."
What he always said was,
"Everybody is the same. Let's all be friends together."
That was all.
So we always did everything together.
Everyone wants a friend, someone to laugh with.
Even starving children
Want to be friends with you.
That is what I wanted to tell you.

AFTERWORD

WHAT I HAVE WRITTEN ABOUT IN THIS BOOK are the things that made the strongest impression on me in the countries I visited. There are lots more things I would like to have written about too. As I did in Tanzania, and mentioned in that chapter, I spent about a hundred hours in each country I went to, being taken to all kinds of places. Naturally, in each country, I was shown schemes they were strongly pursuing, things they were proud of. Nevertheless, eighty-five percent of the world's children live in developing countries like these, and their lives and those of their families are a cause for anxiety. There are only a handful of countries where people live in an environment that provides proper water to drink, health care and education.

From the time I was a child myself, I have liked children. The reason I entered the television and drama world was originally so that I could learn how to read aloud more effectively to children. I am grateful to UNICEF for giving me this work to do. If they had not done so, I probably would have grown old and died without ever knowing about these children in need. How awful that would have been. Had I not been given this work to do, I certainly would have been spared many sad sights and heartbreaking experiences. But now that I know, I can't stop now. "Aren't you discouraged by the hopelessness of it all?" I am often asked, but I am not discouraged.

The former executive director of UNICEF, James P. Grant, told me fourteen million children die every year, and he wanted to cut that figure in half by the end of the century. Alas, we have not been able to halve it, but in fourteen years we have managed to lower the figure to 12.5 million. Even saving the life of one child is a tremendous achievement. And saving even just one child is a far cry from hopelessness.

AFTERWORD

I'd like to take this opportunity to express my heartfelt gratitude to many, many people for their help in fund raising during the past fourteen years. Up to the present time, the end of May 1997, donations received in my UNICEF Goodwill Ambassador Account totaled 2,338,350,768 yen (approximately 22 million dollars). Donations were made by 154,630 individuals and groups. All this money came from you—your kind, generous selves. I would like to write every single one of you a letter saying thank-you from the bottom of my heart, but if I did, I should have to spend 10,657,406 yen (approximately 100,000 dollars) just on stamps!

I'm sure those of you who sent me small but precious donations would not want me to spend the money that way, when 10,657,406 yen would buy enough vaccine to inoculate more than a hundred thousand children against six diseases—measles, TB, polio, diphtheria, tetanus and whooping cough. That stamp money would save vast numbers of lives. I can assure you that all of the money I received has been sent by UNICEF directly to the places where the children are, in the form of things the children need. So please consider your receipt from the bank, or your bank statement, as a proper acknowledgment.

There have been big changes in the world since I was making my visits. First of all, there was the end of the East/West cold war symbolized by the fall of the Berlin Wall in 1989, which affected other countries in various ways. Another was the end of apartheid in South Africa in 1991, and the birth of a black administration with Nelson Mandela as president. This improved conditions somewhat in places like Angola and Mozambique. Freedom has progressed in Vietnam, the economy has improved, and things have livened up to the extent that sightseers are now heading there. Tourist groups can also now visit Angkor Wat in Cambodia.

But there are still countries plagued by poverty and distress.

As I write this, news has just come in of a cyclone in the southeastern part of Bangladesh. The announcer said that, since 1970, 1.5 million people have died as a result of cyclones in this area.

The population of India, which was 772,700,000 when I was there, is now 935,700,000. It has increased that much in just eleven years.

AFTERWORD

As for Zaire, the country to which Rwandan refugees fled, the situation there became such that its president himself had to flee, and in May 1997 its name was changed to the Democratic Republic of Congo.

The backlash from the dispute in Zaire caused a great number of the Rwandans who had taken refuge there to cram themselves into freight cars in a desperate effort to get back to their own country. Evidently, in the stampede, a lot of small children were crushed to death. How awful to be trampled to death, packed tight like that, without knowing why.

Economic sanctions are still in force in Iraq, creating a scarcity of food and medicines, and the situation is serious. The problem of the Kurds is still unsettled.

One hundred and ten million land mines now lie buried among sixty-four countries in the world. It takes a year to remove a hundred thousand of them. At that rate, it will take eleven hundred years to get rid of them all. How can human beings be so foolish? Moreover, each year two million new mines are put into the ground.

I want to tell you about what happened to Benedicta, the little girl at the orphanage in Tanzania. I kept worrying about her, so after I returned to Japan, I corresponded with the Sister at the orphanage, and asked her to start teaching the child English. I sent money for her education. I also asked Mrs. Mongella, the government minister who went to the orphanage with me, if she would keep an eye on the child whenever she had an opportunity to do so.

Four years after I returned from Tanzania, Mrs. Mongella telephoned. "Tetsuko-san," she said, "I know you're interested in Benedicta. Well, our three boys are quite big now, and after talking it over with my husband and them, we decided to adopt her. We're going to give her more or less the same education as the boys. I knew you would be relieved."

I was so surprised, I couldn't think what to say. Mrs. Mongella went on, "She's here now. Just a minute, I'll put her on the phone."

I couldn't stop my tears. To think this lady knew just how I felt. I then heard a tiny little girl's voice on the telephone say, "Hello."

So Benedicta became Mrs. Mongella's daughter, and she has now come out into the world. She lived in India when Mrs. Mongella was ambassador there. And two years ago, in 1995, when Mrs. Mongella was working at the United Nations in New York after being appointed secretary-general of the Beijing World Conference for Women, Benedicta lived there too. I saw Benedicta several times in New York, and the two of us went to musicals together, and ate Japanese food. Although she hasn't been told of our relationship, and remembers nothing herself, she tells me everything, and is attached to me to an almost mysterious degree. Benedicta is modest, and has a lovely voice. She looks rather like a model.

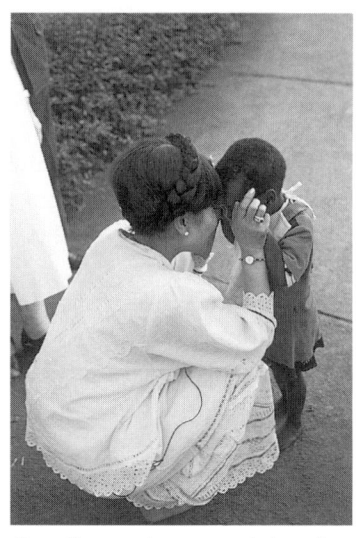

Benedicta, who pressed her face against mine and wouldn't let go.

Her mother talks everything over with me, things such as when Benedicta should be told that she came from an orphanage. We both want her to grow up to be a fine woman. She is back in Tanzania now with Mrs. Mongella, and has started high school. How strange fate is. I hope she will work for the good of Tanzania one day.

It was thanks to Sadako Ogata, the United Nations High Commissioner for Refugees, that I was appointed a goodwill ambassador for UNICEF. Dr. Ogata was a friend of UNICEF's Mr. Grant, and when he asked her to recommend someone from Asia for the post, Dr. Ogata suggested me. Mr. Grant happened to be in Japan just when the English translation of my book *Totto-chan: The Little Girl at the Window* was published, and she gave him a copy. He read it in one night, and then, so he told me, rushed around to all the bookstores in Tokyo and bought as many copies as he could find, which he made everyone in the UNICEF headquarters in New York read. "She certainly understands children" was the general verdict, and that paved the way for my appointment.

AFTERWORD

Meanwhile, Dr. Ogata explained to me about UNICEF. The United Nations was inaugurated in 1945, at the end of the war, and the following year, 1946, UNICEF was founded. At that time, children were starving as a result of the ravages of war in most countries, with a few exceptions such as the United States. Children in Leningrad were said to be reduced to eating wall plaster. Concerned groups in the United States had started sending food to children in Europe. But because Japan and Germany had been enemies, voices were raised that said none need be sent to Japan. The first director-general of UNICEF, however—Maurice Pate—said, "For children, there are neither enemies nor allies," and he saw to it that for thirteen years from 1949 to 1962 about two million dollars worth of suitable goods were sent to us in Japan. Those of us who had powdered milk to drink with our school lunches in those days had it through the kindness of UNICEF.

If we hadn't had that milk, most of the people who keep Japan going today would have suffered from severe malnutrition. At that time, UNICEF had not the slightest idea that Japan would become a country with the second highest GNP in the world. With no thought of return, they were conscious only of the children's needs and provided us with aid. My answer to UNICEF was an immediate "I accept." It wasn't until much later that I heard that UNICEF had been awarded the Nobel Peace Prize.

For fourteen years, whenever I went on a UNICEF inspection tour, Takeyoshi Tanuma, a first-class photographer of children, used to accompany me—at his own expense—with an assistant. Never deterred by the dust of the deserts or the crowds, he used his perceptive eye to produce the superb photographs shown in this book. Ichiro Tagawa, television producer at TV Asahi, also came with me every year, to make special programs with care and sensitivity. And then there is Takashi Hirama, the TV Asahi cameraman who came every year too, lugging his heavy TV camera through thick and thin. Sharp-eyed Hirama never missed a photo opportunity, and has preserved for us on video the images of those innocent children. This team, which seemed to have evolved of itself, was a source of strength and encouragement to me, enabling me to carry out my duties. I also want to thank TV Asahi and all the people who

AFTERWORD

broadcast these programs whenever time permitted. In addition, I am grateful to Nagayo Sawa and Kazuko Uemura, of the UNICEF office in Japan, for their enthusiasm in providing interpreting and for translating from English, and undertaking singlehandedly to provide me with information about children in various parts of the world. If I had not had the help of these two ladies, I would never have been able to write this book. The patience shown by Masanori Yoshizaki of Kodansha was terrific, as was his support, which kept me going when I had fallen way behind my deadline.

Finally, I would like to express my thanks to the journalists and media for their concern for the children of the world, and for the support they have given me. Especially, the late Hitoshi Numazawa, Jin'ichi Matsumoto, Sanae Umezaki, Yuji Yoshikata, Zen Chida, Shizuko Aoki, Toshiyuki Ueno and Hiroshi Kume.

I want to say thank-you too to Mr. Grant who, sadly, died in 1995. He fought the good fight to the end, and gave his life for those children. In the countries I visited there was always a telex message waiting for me from him at the UNICEF office there. I remember them with nostalgia, and sadness: "Tetsuko-san, the children are expecting you. Good luck! And now, what country will you visit next?"

May 1997

POSTSCRIPT

DURING THE THREE YEARS SINCE THIS BOOK was published in Japanese I visited three more countries: Mauritania and Uganda in Africa, as well as Kosovo in Europe—all nations beset with enormous problems.

Mauritania is in the grip of a "silent" crisis as the desert takes away more and more of the land that provided a living for the nomads. These people are being forced to move to the cities, with their proliferating slums, as the towns and villages where they used to live disappear into the sand.

There is nothing for miles but desert and barren wasteland. In its midst, you see patches of leafy greenery which look like oases. But the trees are poisonous. Any animals that try to eat the leaves die. If a child picks a leaf, and the juice gets in its eyes, the child goes blind. It is a tree that needs little water to grow and prosper, and produces none of the water vapor essential for making rain. It is truly a devil's tree. One wonders what on earth can be the purpose of such a plant.

And yet, with all its problems, there are people who love the desert, and contrive all sorts of schemes for keeping the sands at bay. The handsome governor—who would make a perfect Othello in Shakespeare's play—was supporting research into varieties of rice and tomato that could be harvested three times a year. He was also busy encouraging people to use insecticide-treated mosquito nets to prevent malaria. Everyone was working as hard as they could. It was gratifying to meet so many people who refused to give up the struggle.

As for Uganda, a third of that country was being terrorized by armed guerrillas who abducted boys and girls of indoctrinable age, between eleven and sixteen. The children were given military training and taught to shoot their own countrymen. Besides fighting, the girls were forced to become the wives of the guerrillas. A woman whose daughter had been kidnapped at fourteen, and whose whereabouts she didn't know, told me she had seen a girl of about fifteen, with a baby on her back, firing a gun at the village in which she used to live. The woman said it was like a scene from hell. She still hoped her daughter would return one day, and her eyes were red from crying.

Uganda is one of the countries with the largest number of children made orphans by AIDS: 1.1 million, or one in nine. As a result of concerted national efforts there have been fewer new cases, but nevertheless, ten percent of the adult population is HIV/AIDS infected.

There were also a great many street children. But in spite of that, Uganda seemed serious about promoting education, and children appeared to be doing well at elementary school. I asked some elementary school pupils in Kampala, the capital, "If I could grant you any wish, what would your wish be?" One boy said without hesitation, "I'd like the war between Pakistan and India to stop." How many elementary school children in Japan would even understand that boy's wish? Japan is closer to India and Pakistan than Uganda, yet there, in faroff Africa, children felt strongly about the issue! I told the principal of the school how impressed I was.

I visited Kosovo last summer just as most of the refugees from the armed conflict were finally returning to their homes. Most of the buildings had been razed, and you had to pick your way through rubble. Land mines lay buried everywhere, and there were many child casualties. The first thing they taught at school was about mines. Waving aloft a can of the childrens' favorite soft drink, a teacher asked, "What would you do if you found one of these in a field?" A boy replied, "I would tell a grown-up." "Correct," the teacher replied. Then, holding up a carton, the teacher asked a little girl what she would do if she saw one of these lying around. The child inquired promptly, "What's in it?" When the teacher told her it was orange juice, the little girl replied that if it was orange juice, she'd go a bit closer and make sure. But go any closer and the mine would explode. The child would be killed. Orange juice was hard to come by, so it was very tempting for a child. "No! No! Quite wrong!" cried the teacher. "You'd never find a real carton of orange juice lying in a field."

The teacher was frantic. There were so many booby traps like that aimed specifically at children. I heard that a million land mines lay buried throughout Kosovo, and I felt so sad when I thought of myself as a child and how I used to jump about with glee in any grassy field I came across. I want children to know about Kosovo—children who live in countries where they can run about wherever they please without having to worry about explosions.

I shall never forget the story told to me by a university professor I met in Kosovo. Some men suddenly appeared with guns and said he must leave Kosovo right away. He was taken to a railway station, where children and adults were being separated into different trains, and as the trains moved off in opposite directions, visions of Auschwitz flashed across adult minds. "We're all going to be killed," they thought. It was raining. The train stopped, and they were told to get out and walk the rest of the way. They had to cross a minefield, but finally reached a refugee camp from which my professor friend eventually came back to Kosovo alive. Some of his cousins had been killed, and his house and everything else had been destroyed. But he had survived, and was now starting a second life, he told me, his voice full of vim and vigor.

To start a new life after the age of sixty is quite an undertaking. But when you think of all the people who have seen their parents killed before their very eyes, people in camps separated from their families, children left in camps not knowing that their parents have been killed, what else is there to do but to go on, looking toward the future, like the university professor?

It was impossible to count the number of children left with psychological scars. One girl told me she had seen her father shot. Actually he was still alive—he had simply fallen, cleverly feigning death. But even though he was right there with her, able to hold and comfort her, when night fell she was so sure he was dead she could never sleep for more than an hour. That was the kind of living nightmare children had to cope with.

After returning from these three additional tours, I told listeners about them as I always do in my various television programs: a one-and-a-half-hour special program; my daily talk show, "Tetsuko's Room" (which is now in its twenty-fifty year); and a highly popular news program—all of which reach a wide audience.

By the end of May, the total amount of contributions from kind listeners had reached a fantastic new total of 3,045,838,083 yen (about $26,000,000) received from 212,550 individuals and groups! The money has already gone off to UNICEF and is being used right now to help children suffering the greatest hardships. The grim fact is that three years on, in this millennium year, fighting still continues in many regions.

But I must tell you about Benedicta. Last year Benedicta was married. And this year she became a mother. Mrs. Mongella says the baby girl is adorable, and looks just like Benedicta. A few years ago Mrs. Mongella and I talked it over and decided that when she was seventeen we would tell Benedicta about finding her at the orphanage, in case she had any doubts or questions lingering in her mind. Mrs. Mongella took Benedicta to the orphanage. But they arrived at the wrong one by mistake. "This isn't it," said Benedicta, and led the way to the right one. So the memory was there after all! "This is where I used to live," said Benedicta. "But I'm still your daughter, Mom."

I am so happy that Benedicta has grown into a fine young woman, and what exciting news about the baby. Mrs. Mongella and I now have a grandchild. How strange a tie it is that binds us!

And now there is this wonderful English edition of my book, thanks to Dorothy Britton, who translated my *Totto-chan: The Little Girl at the Window* so ably. I am thrilled to think that people in many countries will be able to read it. I wish I could tell all the children I've met that the people reading this book will surely be thinking about them. And that there's a UNICEF goodwill ambassador in Japan who worries about them night and day, and rejoices if the number of children who manage to face the future with hope increases even just by one.

What a long PS this has become. Thank you for reading it all.

August 2000 (as I leave for Liberia,
which has been in a state of turmoil
for the past seven years.)

UNICEF GOODWILL AMBASSADORS

UNICEF (an acronym of the United Nations International Children's Emergency Fund, now shortened to the United Nations Children's Fund) is mandated by the United Nations General Assembly to advocate for the protection of children's rights, to help meet their basic needs and to expand their opportunities to reach their full potential. In approximately 160 countries, UNICEF works with other United Nations agencies, governments and non-governmental organizations to provide community-based services in primary health care, nutrition, basic education and safe water and sanitation to the developing world.

UNICEF currently has six goodwill ambassadors, personal representatives of the UNICEF executive director, volunteering their time and talents to draw the public's attention to the needs of children in developing countries. They receive an annual salary of one dollar.

The late Danny Kaye pioneered the role as UNICEF's first ambassador at large. He was followed by the producer, novelist, playwright and actor Sir Peter Ustinov and Norwegian actress, Liv Ullmann. Tetsuko Kuroyanagi, the popular Japanese actress and television personality became UNICEF's fourth goodwill ambassador in 1984. Harry Belafonte, the singer, Lord Attenborough, who became familiar with UNICEF's work while making the film *Ghandi* in India, the late Audrey Hepburn and 007 star Roger Moore are the others.

In 1987 Tetsuko Kuroyanagi was awarded the first UNICEF Child Survival Award.

Readers who wish to contribute to UNICEF through Tetsuko Kuroyanagi's goodwill ambassador account in Tokyo can send money to:

UNICEF GOODWILL AMBASSADOR TETSUKO KUROYANAGI
Account No. #1546555
Dai-ichi Kangyo Bank, Roppongi Branch, Tokyo.

For information on how you can help UNICEF please contact the U.S. Fund for UNICEF, Department 1220N, P.O. Box 97295, Washington, DC 20090-7295, call 1-800-FOR-KIDS or access to **www.unicefusa.org**.

Part of the royalties from the sale of this book will be used for UNICEF causes.

トットちゃんとトットちゃんたち
TOTTO-CHAN'S CHILDREN

2000年8月9日 第1刷発行

著 者　黒柳　徹子
訳 者　ドロシー・ブリトン
装幀者　和田　誠
発行者　野間佐和子
発行所　講談社インターナショナル株式会社
　　　　〒112-8652　東京都文京区音羽 1-17-14
　　　　電話：03-3944-6493（編集部）
　　　　　　　03-3944-6492（業務部・営業部）
印刷所　共同印刷株式会社
製本所　黒柳製本株式会社

落丁本、乱丁本は、講談社インターナショナル業務部宛にお送りください。送料小社負担にてお取替えいたします。なお、この本についてのお問い合わせは、編集部宛にお願いいたします。本書の無断複写（コピー）は著作権法上での例外を除き、禁じられています。

定価はカバーに表示してあります。

Copyright © 1997 by Tetsuko Kuroyanagi
English translation copyright © 2000 by Kodansha International Ltd.
ISBN 4-7700-2532-7